Dim Sum 1

Dim Sum for Managers

Advice and Ideas for the Hungry Mind

Adrian Furnham

CYANBOOKS

Copyright © 2008 Adrian Furnham

First published in 2008 by:

Cyan Communications Limited
Fifth Floor (Marshall Cavendish)
32–38 Saffron Hill
London EC1N 8FH
United Kingdom
T: +44 (0)20 7421 8145
F: +44 (0)20 7421 8121
sales@cyanbooks.com
www.cyanbooks.com

A CIP record for this book is available from the British Library

ISBN-13 978-1-904879-94-7
ISBN-10 1-904879-94-2

Typeset by Phoenix Photosetting, Chatham, Kent

Printed and bound in Great Britain by
CPI Bookmarque, Croydon CR0 4TD

Contents

Contents

Introduction

'Shall we get together for dim sum? Tapas? Sushi? Meze?'
Many cultures, it seems, have the same concept: a range of
dishes offered in small helpings, each with its individual
taste, which, taken as a whole, make a substantial meal. They
are a celebration of variety, of difference, but also of compat-
ibility. They are often attractively served. They can be taken
at any time of day. And because eating is always, and in every
culture, a social event, the idea is that the food nourishes the
body and the convivial company nourishes the mind.

Dim sum is food for all seasons. It can be obtained from
home or bought in. Or one can find it in the bustle of a busy
restaurant. It is fuel to sustain life; but it is always attractively
presented.

While there is no total agreement about the history and
meaning of dim sum, there are few people who do not
believe this sort of Chinese brunch is a wonderful invention.
It originated in the province of Canton. It is *dien sing* in
Mandarin. It has been variously described as 'small choices
of the heart' or 'heart's delight.' Some say it means 'pointing
to your heart's desires' as carts of tempting food pass by. The
dishes maximize flavor and variety. They are of different
shapes and textures: some sweet, some savory, some salty. It
is believed that, since the tenth century, as many as 2000
different varieties of dim sum have evolved.

In many Chinese restaurants dim sum is served most of
the day, often to people in large groups at large tables.
Restaurants are constantly busy and noisy, with continual
throughput. Frequently, servers push carts or trolleys full of
carry trays with their hot, freshly cooked wares. Each has a
set price and their check/card might be stamped by the

passing waiters. It is not, nor does it pretend to be, fine dining. Waiters are in a hurry. They do not specialize in charming service. They prize efficiency and turnaround more than charm or courtesy. And the diners like it that way.

Usually diners start with lighter steamed dishes, followed by more exotic and unusual offerings (chicken's feet, duck's tongues), then more substantial deep-fried foods and, finally, dessert ... all washed down with generous amounts of tea. Hence the term *yum cha*, which means a meal accompanied by tea, to include *tso cha* (morning meal) and *an cha* (afternoon tea).

But the Chinese are not unique at inventing a menu of this type. So we also have Middle Eastern meze, Spanish tapas, Swedish smorgasbord, Italian antipasti and Japanese sushi.

Tapas vary according to region and season, and, like dim sum, their eating is a very social occasion. People from all walks of life gather together for refreshment and social contact. It is a meal that can be eaten standing up or sitting down.

The Swedish smorgasbord is usually a buffet with many small dishes to choose from. Then there is sushi, the Japanese version. There are now in many countries those unique restaurants with elaborate tracks that allow small, beautifully prepared rice and fish dishes to travel past hungry and admiring patrons perched on stools, eager to choose the ones that most appeal.

There are, of course, differences in the ingredients of these cultural dishes: some are more rice oriented, some more grain focused. Some are predominantly served cold, others hot. Some are usually accompanied by alcohol, others rarely so. Some are associated with social occasions and relaxation, others with work. But they have more in common than they differ.

As the world shrinks and people travel they take their

recipes and ingredients with them. Others discover exotic flavors and styles, and rejoice in them. So its not unusual to see in big international cities like New York and Hong Kong, London and Paris, Singapore and Berlin, a street that has restaurants offering dim sum, tapas, meze and sushi literally next door to one another. And there may be as many people of European origin enjoying the dim sum and sushi as there are people of Asian origin enjoying the tapas or meze.

There are some universals in taste as there are universals in people. And the way we rate, judge, and consume food is often merely superficially different.

Meals as management metaphors

This book contains just over 80 short essays: tasty bites of business knowledge. These essays are, I believe, a little like the contents of dim sum (or tapas). They have qualities in common, as outlined below.

Anytime (any place)

Just as dim sum can be consumed morning, noon, and night, there are always opportunities to learn. Air and rail journeys are good examples of the sort of 'downtime' that can be used for learning. Learning, advice, and knowledge are not confined to classrooms during periods of education. Meals are social events: people tell stories, shoot the breeze, chat. They tell of their experiences and their perceptions. Most of us learn better in groups, and we learn by doing. You learn to cook in groups, by trial and error. And you never stop learning—nor should you. Dim sum can, and should, be consumed whenever people gather and are hungry. Hungry for company, for ideas, for sharing.

Balanced diet

Too much of anything is bad for you. Dim sum rejoices in variety and balance. We like to eat savory and sweet. We need food with fiber and vitamins. And we like to enjoy our favorite treats. The same is true of business knowledge. We need to know many things about the business world. Business is complex. People are complex. The workforce is increasingly diverse. One size, one theory, one management style does not fit all. Most people these days strive for a work–life balance. This concept is important: too much of anything is bad for you. There are few foods that are really bad for you; the issue lies in *how frequently* they are consumed and *how much* they are consumed.

A monotonous, homogenous diet is both boring and bad for you. We need a balance of vitamins for health. And so it is for work: 'All work and no play makes Jack a dull boy,' as the saying goes. But all play and no work is not much better. The trick is balance.

Body and soul (head and heart)

Food is more than sustenance for the body: it pleases the soul. There is comfort food and healthy food. But its origin and rarity, and the way it is presented and served please the eye, the head, and the heart. More importantly, the way it is consumed is important. Everyone knows that food is more than just fuel. It has associations. It can be symbolic. There are rare foods and sacred foods. There are foods to *sustain life* and foods to *enhance life*.

Cooks say we eat with our eyes as much as our mouths. But we eat together. A satisfying meal satisfies many needs at the same time. We don't work just for the money. Good work fulfils other needs. It gives one a sense of identity and it is a source of friends and companions. It also allows us to play to our strengths. It should be psychologically, socially, and physically, satisfying.

Complementarity

Dim sum dishes complement each other. They complement the tea served. They are insufficient on their own but together form a fine meal. And dim sum, tapas, meze, and the like, can precede a formal main meal. It is not only brave and clever cooks that know about complementary and unexpected combinations. Thus while some people serve strawberries with cream and sugar, it is believed the best things to put on strawberries to enhance and draw out their flavor are vinegar and pepper.

We have known for a long time that opposites can attract because they can complement each other's preferences and skills. The impulsive and the obsessive, the introvert and the extrovert, the creative and the practical need each other. They complement each other and bring to bear their natural strengths and preferences. And so it is, or should be, in the workplace. A thoughtfully combined, diverse work team functions best.

Cookery book

Dim sum chefs possibly start off with a cookbook, carefully following the lists of ingredients and processes described. People can learn from cookbooks or from watching and working for great cooks. But they also learn by intuition. One moves from reading books, to experimenting, to writing books about cookery. So it is with management. There are management cookbooks. They offer simple dishes—often simplistic dishes. There is no shortage of silver-bullet, magic-solution business books that offer the formula or solution to all problems.

Cookery books and management books are the way you start to learn. They set out some basic principles rather attractively. Often the ideas are simple but effective. And the books are very repetitive. Despite the number printed and published, few cookery books have new recipes. They usually repackage old ones or, likely, introduce the food of a different region or country.

Surprisingly few cooks read cookery books. And surprisingly few managers need orthodox management books. Once past basic principles they learn by experience.

Flavorsome

Dim sum, tapas, and meze rejoice in the variety and intensity of different flavors that can be combined in various ways. People have one thing in common: they are all different. Flavor comes from clever, often unusual, combinations, the sort that make a highly productive, but heterogeneous team.

Apart from the way food is served there are a few essential qualities that make food both distinctive and desirable. One is texture, but perhaps more important is flavor.

Because supermarkets in the West demand so much consistency of shape, color, and texture to fruit and vegetables, they appear to overlook that most crucial of factors: taste. It is as if this is less important.

It is not an uncommon experience for environmentally conscious consumers to buy small, perhaps misshapen, but perfectly ripe fruit or vegetables from a farmers' market. What strikes one is the intensity of flavor. It is as if the perfectly formed, symmetrical, equal-sized fruit and vegetables from the local supermarket have been drained of their very essence: their flavor.

Furthermore, in the process of cooking many ingredients are pulped or puréed, or diced, so that their shape is far less important than their flavor.

The flavor of an organization could be thought of as its corporate culture. Strong flavors are strong cultures. They can represent the essence of an organization.

For sharing

Dim sum is for sharing, and so are management skills. Management education is good for people. Every organization wants an adaptive, healthy corporate culture, where assumption and values are shared, and where people are nicely aligned to attain specific goals.

Management is a contact sport. We are social animals. We need each other. Hence all the emphasis on teamwork, particularly in the individualistic cultures of the West.

But more than that we need, at work, alignment. We need to be geared up to reach the same goal. And therefore we need information, and more particularly feedback, on how we are doing.

Management techniques, management ideas, management philosophy have to be shared. These things are worthless if they are unknown. Employees have shared goals and, it is to be hoped, shared values. Sharing is about understanding each other, our values and purpose. It is as miserable to eat alone as to work alone. Solitary confinement is, after all, a punishment. We need convivial social contact.

Fresh

Dim sum is made with fresh produce. Ideas, technology, and values can become out of date. Management education is all about updating organizations and changing them to be able to deal with the environment in which they operate.

Cooks talk about 'refreshing' a salad. They talk about the value of just caught, or just picked produce. They know that frozen or canned produce may well be second best.

Ideas and management practices can be frozen. Technology, techniques, and processes can be terribly out of date.

There is a great difference between a fresh approach and a faddish approach, although they may look very similar. Managers are prone to fads—they suffer from the 'tyranny of the new' just as much as the 'tyranny of the urgent.'

A fresh tomato, a fresh shrimp, a fresh orange is much better than one that is stale. Ideas have their own sell-by dates. Organizations and managers need refreshing: this may involve going on sabbaticals; it may involve calling in consultants; it may involve a bit of blue-sky thinking.

Hot and cold

Most dim sum dishes are hot, but not all. The same is true of tapas and hors d'oeuvres. Some people think of hot and cold as the heart (hot, passionate, seat of emotion) and the head (cold, rational, seat of logic). Both are important and necessary in business. Both have their place, both contribute to the overall pattern.

People, they say, can blow hot and cold. This means that they express alternately great and little enthusiasm for projects. But hot and cold have further meaning. The yin and yang differentiate between hot and cold foods, not in terms of their temperature, but their effects. The (cold, raw) mango is among the hottest of foods, while warm boiled rice is cool.

Some ideas are hot; some people are hot. And some can be too hot. Ideas can be tepid and they can be lukewarm. And so can enthusiasm. Many meals celebrate hot and cold food. This is very true of dim sum, but more so of meze and tapas. One can have a tastebud-refreshing sorbet between two flavorsome hot dishes. It adds variety.

Revenge, they say, is a dish best served cold. And cold people are thought of as unattractive. But there is the role of the cool head in turbulent times, and the importance of a clinical, cool, and dispassionate evaluation of a complex situation.

Nourishing

Dim sum is a nourishing meal. A varied diet means that you are more likely to find the trace elements and vitamins, fats and proteins that the body needs. In the same way, managers need to be exposed to a variety of ideas, techniques, and processes in order to be able to pick the most appropriate for their organization. A monotonous or unbalanced diet won't do. And the mind, the soul, and the body all need nourishing.

One needs to feed the mind and feed the soul. Some foods are more nourishing than others. To nourish means to nurture, to encourage, to grow and to foster. To nourish is to cherish. Nourishing food is that which provides the essential materials (minerals, vitamins) necessary for a healthy life and growth. This may be all the more necessary at certain times. Young children, pregnant women, older people, and those recovering from illness are rightly encouraged to pay careful attention to the food they eat.

Managers need to nourish supervisors, who need to manage staff. They need information and emotional support. They need the tools to finish the job. The questions remain: 'Who nourishes the nurturer?,' 'Who feeds the cook?'

This book is meant to nourish and to help growth. It encourages people to challenge old ideas and old ways. It encourages people to try something different.

Signature dishes

Some cooks and restaurants have a signature dish. This means something they do exceptionally well, that they would like others to judge them by. Organizations also hope to strive to be different, to have areas of great expertise and excellence that distinguish them from the rest.

To be particularly good at something is always desirable. To make something one's own is healthy. Organizations protect their brand fiercely. They like to be known as special, as having something that is particularly good—the best in the world.

Cooks and restaurants often enjoy being known for a particular dish. Often it is a traditional dish but with a re-interpretation of ingredients, style and presentation. The cook is attempting to demonstrate his or her skill, imagination, even humor. It is, they hope, the source (and sauce) of their reputation.

Equally, managers may consciously acquire a style, a quirk, a unique way of doing things that is akin to a signature dish. As long as it is functional and desirable it is inevitably a very good thing.

Varied

Dim sum, smorgasbord, antipasti, and the like, celebrate variety. They are the 'pick and mix' of the food world. There is bound to be something everybody likes … and quite possibly that some do not like. Variety is indeed the spice of life. True of food. True of business.

There is, inevitably, tension between being consistent and being varied. Many organizations really struggle with consistency of service and consistency of product. Customers value consistency of standards as well as variety of choice. They like to know what they are getting, they like variety and, often, novelty.

Dim sum at a particularly favored restaurant is frequently a celebration of consistency of variety. The dim sum is always good. And there are many varied dishes. This is what we are often trying to achieve in business.

Introduction

This book offers a dim sum approach to management concepts. Each chapter stands on its own to be read individually, but as part of a menu. It hopes to feed the management mind, to offer a satisfying, nutritious, varied meal of tasty bites to be savored individually or in combination. Like dim sum they are international in their appeal; they are (I hope) easy to digest, and they require no filleting.

Absence makes you wonder

What do national absenteeism statistics tell us about the nature of this phenomenon? The 2005 Confederation of British Industry (CBI) survey of 522 British organizations revealed the following information.

- The average number of days lost is nearly seven per annum per employee.
- There is a slight trend downwards.
- Absenteeism in the public sector is a third higher than in the private sector.
- Absenteeism goes up as organizations get bigger.
- Organizations that don't recognize unions have fewer absences.
- Absence is higher among manual vs non-manual employees.
- The direct cost of absence is about £500 per employee to his/her organization.
- Employers believe that up to one-fifth of absenteeism is not genuine.
- If senior managers, as opposed to line managers, were in charge of absenteeism it was reduced by one-third.
- Absence management can work wonders, but it takes many forms.

Absenteeism is one of those topics—a bit like performance-related pay—that immediately divides people. Unlike some areas, like appraisals or accidents, which see overall consensus, the cause and cures of absenteeism split people into very different camps. They can easily, perhaps inaccurately, be labeled 'capitalist–socialist,' 'greedy vs compassionate' and 'naive vs realistic.'

One side takes a management perspective, the other a labor perspective. The latter sees absences arising from stress and illness, or work–life imbalance, or inefficient management and poor conditions. They look at poorly paid, unskilled public-sector workers with little job satisfaction, little self-actualization, and poor prospects. They see their work as monotonous. They see their prospects as poor. They see their managers as uncaring, or manipulative, or themselves absenting. And they don't blame them. Some organizations have replaced the concept of 'taking a sickie' with having a mental health day. This is all part of *Nineteen Eighty-Four*-type newspeak, where failure is now 'delayed success,' stress is 'challenge,' and weaknesses are 'developmental opportunities.' This is not only dangerous but foolish. If absenteeism is called health, this implies that work causes illness!

The management perspective does not always 'blame' the worker, but it is not prepared to accept that all, even the majority, of absenteeism, is genuine. It sees many workers as opportunistic shirkers. It notices the patterns in absenteeism and concludes that people are simply increasing their vacation allowance.

But it also blames poor, weak, or inadequate line supervisors for not dealing with the problem. The central question remains how best to tackle the issue, which can be costly to the individual, his/her peers, and the organization as a whole. There are many possible tactics: employ some occupational health experts; financially reward presenteeism (like having a no-claims bonus); try running a training program.

Some approaches work better than others. First, put the issue on the table, high on the agenda for everybody. Make the issue explicit—get everybody to talk about the causes, but more importantly the solutions. The more *everybody* agrees a policy to deal with the issues, the more likely they are to follow the prescribed behavior. Agreed guidelines are essential.

Next, line managers but also senior (HR) managers need to have explicit responsibility for managing and probably reducing absenteeism. They need to model the behavior—by their own record—as well as doing specific things. These include conducting return-to-work interviews, visiting chronic absenters at their homes, having thorough appraisals. They need to bite the bullet early and not let things drag on. They need to know and fully implement disciplinary procedures. They need to measure and document absenteeism, and share the information with supervisors and staff.

They need to show compassion where appropriate, but also firmness where there is faking. Occupational health experts have to understand fully the benefits and necessity of a successful, present organization, and the cost of absence.

And, of course, when selecting people their history of absenteeism needs to be investigated. There is acute and chronic absenteeism, and it is the latter that is more important. People who are frequently absent may be particularly stress prone, chronically ill, or easily inclined to take time off 'sick.' This merits serious consideration right from the very beginning.

Accentuate the positive

In the old days the lay person's idea of strategic planning could be boiled down to four relatively simple steps. First, you did a brutally frank, objective analysis of who, where, and why you (the organization) were at the point you were. This could be pretty depressing but was considered essential. It was a reality check. You had to confront reality and own up to your 'manifold sins and wickedness.' Not all doom and gloom, of course, but usually a call to action.

Then you painted a picture of where you wanted to be. This was usually more uplifting as an exercise, but one was constantly reminded to be realistic, to take into consideration changes in the customers, the workforce, and the competition. Futurology can be fun. It can waken the optimism in one. It can help the creative juices flow. Only the old, sour, and bitter are nihilistically pessimistic at this phase.

The third phase was to try to list all the forces that were on your side. That is, the factors that would facilitate the happy metamorphosis from current (grim) state to that (highly desired) future state. The list may be long or short, and could include any set of factors, from the quality and quantity of your workers to the brand reputation.

Sometimes the list of positive factors looked pathetically thin and weak. Often they could be boiled down to one or two, which included luck as a major feature. Sometimes they seemed more about competitors' weaknesses than one's own strength, or more statements of fact about the market. And, very occasionally, the list was so long and robust that all one hoped for was the status quo in perpetuity.

The fourth and final phase was to identify the list of factors—economic, psychological, physical, historical, and such like—that prevented or inhibited one reaching the promised land of plenty, profit, and prosperity. Like mapping the present, this could all get rather gloomy as the list grew and grew. But there you are.

Having drawn your map you were then encouraged to focus on the negative, the restraining forces, those factors that supposedly prevented one from reaching one's desired goals. The idea was to attack the virus, eliminate the cancers, destroy the enemies (within and without). One had to pinpoint the problems and attack them systematically with energy and focus.

The idea was that the strengths would remain and it was the weaknesses that had to be attacked. Then two things happened. First, the PC, anti-pessimistic thought-police banned all negative language. No one, no group, no organization had weaknesses: they had developmental opportunities; setbacks, handicaps, and failures were to be rebranded in the somewhat naive belief that this would help people deal with them.

Then the world changed, some time around the millennium, we saw the birth of positive psychology, and the whole focus changed. The spotlight was moved from the dark to the light. From the can't do to the can do and from weakness to strength. People were encouraged to concentrate on the potential of strengths such as optimism, creativity, and kindness, to enhance happiness, efficacy, and adaptability at the individual and organizational level.

Positive people live longer and have more life and job satisfaction. Positive organizations have less absenteeism, fewer accidents, and greater productivity.

So the whole emphasis shifted to boosting the immune system. It was and is a sort of alternative medicine. It is a celebration of strengths not an investigation into weakness.

The process now starts with positives. Without hubris or bias you are encouraged to investigate—on an individual, group, and organizational level—your strengths and how to boost them. So you are encouraged to be thankful and to teach others how to be likewise.

Furthermore a positive mental attitude is thought to be amazingly healthy and self-fulfilling. Thus optimism begets success as much as pessimism does failure. Cardinal virtues are talked about in business seminars. And we hear about forgiveness and trust and joy, and words heard more commonly in the pulpit than on the PowerPoint slide. There is more emphasis on emotion than in the old days. Heart has replaced head. And this chimes terribly well with all the interest in emotional intelligence.

So is the coldly analytic, problem-solving strategist a thing of the past? Did they do themselves and their client organizations a massive disservice by focusing on all the wrong things? Or is this simply the pendulum swinging back slightly? Only time will tell.

Advice for young managers

How do you 'get on' at work? Apart from hard work and exploiting natural ability and emotional intelligence, what is the best way to climb the greasy corporate pole to senior manager and board director level?

The two central tasks for anyone in the workplace are getting along with and getting ahead of your peers. The question is, how is this best achieved?

What advice should wise, been-there-done-that senior executives give to their younger colleagues? Indeed what do they say to their sons and daughters at the appropriate time to help them benefit from their experience?

Advice of this sort no doubt comes in various versions. One version is the bland, chin-up school of 'do your best,' 'play up, play up and play the game.' Others might indulge in the most wicked cynicism, suggesting various unethical, casting-couch-type techniques to achieve one's ends.

For those genuinely interested in this issue the central question is whether the strategy depends on the organization. In short, should the advice be different depending on whether it is aimed at people in big vs small, private vs public sector, tall vs flat organizations … or is it the same for all?

While it may be true that corporate culture does affect style, it probably does not powerfully influence content. So what are the seven secrets of successful young people at work?

1. As quickly as possible become, or at least appear to be, indispensable

Having a skill set that others need and don't possess is a wonderful asset. In the land of the blind and all that, being the only person to speak Malay, or understand Excel, or nurture a temperamental machine or person, gives one special status. So the advice is to explore your particular talents and hone those that the organization wants and that are in short supply. Equally, seek out organizations that value your particular skill-set. They really need to need your skills.

2. Always be a committed, open, enthusiastic team player

Learn to cooperate, to include others, to be supportive. Because we come from an individualistic culture we invest a lot of time and energy in learning to be collectivistic. Sadistic ex-military types find employment in outdoor boot camps teaching middle-aged middle managers with middle-age spread to be team players. Real team players are rare, helpful, and therefore valuable. Stress the 'we' over the 'I.'

3. Work out the real power structure, establish useful alliances, and find soulmates

Get connected and embedded throughout the organization. You never know when you might need allies, helpers, and supporters. Get out of your silo and do your own matrix organization. Understand, through relationships, how the whole organization works. Never believe the organizational chart. Informal leaders are very influential. Find them. Charm them. Befriend them.

4. Be positive, don't whine, and never get caught gossiping

It is the alienated, passed over, and irritated that spend their life sniping. They are often angry about the past, gloomy about the future, and disenchanted with the present. Their negativity and nyet-ness sucks the air and energy out of meetings, colleagues, and customers. Positive people, by contrast, are life enhancing, fun to be around, and at the heart of a good party. Do 'can' and not 'can't,' and see the upside first, long before the downside.

5. Know when to attract and avoid the limelight

Make sure you get noticed by the right people at the right time, but don't overdo it. There is little worse than an egocentric attention-seeking, narcissistic young person whose self-obsession is very off-putting. Less is sometimes more. It is better to give a few brilliant presentations than many competent ones. Pick your opportunities, prepare to the point that everything looks natural and easy, and praise others when they have done well.

6. Manage up and across as well as down

We know from 360-degree feedback (or multi-rater ratings) that, paradoxically, of all the people who come into contact with you, your boss knows you least well. Your staff know about your management style, your colleagues about your abilities, and your boss about the consequences of your style. You have to beat your colleagues to get your boss's job, so make sure he or she is kept well briefed on all you want him or her to know.

7. Keep your options open, your CV updated, and your skill-set sharp

The career is not dead. But snakes-and-ladders behavior may be required to do well. You may have to leave the organization and rejoin to overcome some obstacles ahead. So welcome head-hunters, read the appointments pages, know your market value. And, where necessary, update your skills and knowledge.

Of course, not everybody would agree with the above. Cynics say all the game playing is insincere and one gets found out pretending. Maybe. But corporate life is a struggle.

MANAGEMENT DESIDERATA

Once it was called 'work satisfaction,' then 'commitment,' and now 'engagement.' Its opposite is 'alienation,' estranged from all that happens in the workplace.

All managers want their staff to be fully committed to the aims of the organization, happy in their work and totally engaged in what they are doing. So how to achieve engagement? Indeed, is it even possible to engage people doing unskilled, dreary, repetitive work? And is engagement an end in itself, or does it lead to other desirable outcomes such as productivity, profitability, staff retention, and customer satisfaction?

The research in this area shows pretty consistent findings. The results are neither surprising nor counterintuitive. And they have been known for ages. So why is it that supervisors and managers do not perform their duties so as to maximize the commitment and engagement of their staff?

There are some fairly basic but important things a manager needs to do to maximize engagement. They are presented here as a checklist, Management 101, a desiderata for the director/decision-maker/desktop.

- Let every person know what is expected of them in terms of their processes and products. Be clear. Check understandings. And revisit expectations as they change. All people have hopes and expectations about promotion, about change, about what their organization should be doing for them (and they for the organization). These expectations need to be managed.
- Give people the tools for the job. Keep them up to date. Train them how to use these tools. Make sure that processes are well thought through so that the technology people use is appropriate for what they are required to do. In short, give technical and informational support.
- Give people opportunities to learn and shine at what they are good at. People like to celebrate their skills, abilities, and unique gifts. Help them find and explore

them. Let them do their best all the time. And encourage development of strengths.

♦ Be generous but targeted in praise. Recognize effort and success. Recognize individuals and how they strive to achieve. Celebrate success. Notice and praise individuals when they have put in extra effort. And do it openly, naturally, and regularly.

♦ Listen to your employees. They often have very good and innovative ideas. Yes, they can and do complain, but listen to that too. They need to believe their ideas count, their voice is heard, they can contribute to how the work is arranged.

♦ Help them believe in the purpose or product of the organization. People need to feel their job is important; that they really are making a contribution to society. This involves more than writing fancy mission statements. It's about giving the job a sense of meaning and purpose.

♦ Encourage friendship formation at work. This is more than insisting on teamwork. It is giving people space and time to build up a friendship network. Friends are a major source of social support. They make all the difference to the working day. And committed people commit their friends.

♦ Talk to people about their progress. Give them a chance to let off steam, to dream about what might be, to have quality time with you. This is more than those detailed, often rather forced appraisals. It is about opportunity for the boss to focus on the hopes, aspirations, and plans of the individual.

Pretty obvious stuff. Be clear about what you want. That is, define the outcomes required for individuals that will strengthen and challenge them. Focus on what they do well: their strengths, gifts, and talents. Try to find the best individual and the best in the individual. Make them exemplars, heroes, models. Find the right fit between a person's talents and ambitions and the tasks they need to do.

Look for ambitious, achievement-oriented, energetic individuals. But steer their striving: manage their route map. And look for, listen to and reward evidence of independent ideas and thinking. Never assume management has a monopoly on the truth. Also encourage camaraderie: help people who are social animals relate to each other and pull together.

Do all of the above and you have an engaged workforce. And we do know that happy, healthy staff treat customers better. It's a relatively simply causal link. It pays to focus on staff engagement. But it's also the fundamental task of all management. Amen!

Business alumni

It is our custom to give people a good send-off. This is nicely manifested in the funeral wake, where friends, family, and acquaintances gather to pay their respects, recall the past, offer their thanks, and so on.

Business retirement occasions also recognize a passing: a passing from employed to unemployed status; from the day job to the potting shed; from twice as much time to half as much pay.

There are many mixed emotions at retirement parties. And, of course, it's not only the leaver who ponders the past and the future. It is also his/her boss, colleagues, subordinates, etc., particularly those close in age to the retiree.

And it is not so much how, when, and why people are 'let go,' but how you treat them afterwards that is important. Schools and colleges are very aware of their past pupils, and for good reason. They can be a source of extensive wealth and good will. Top colleges dedicate considerable resources to alumni magazines, meetings, and memorabilia merchandising to keep those memories sweet. For every dollar spent ten may flow back into the organization.

Some educational institutions are so keen on the idea that even if you attend only a short course at their establishment with no examination or diploma at the end you are still treated like an alumnus. You bathe in the light of the institutions just as much as PhD students. And nobody seems to mind. Everyone gains.

Alumni act not only as potential donors but also as excellent marketers. They can become excellent ambassadors and champions of the brand, spreading the news of the educational excellence of the institution to friends and relations, and they even bang the drum overseas. Free and very good publicity.

But more than anything they provide a forum for contact. Most people wish to keep in touch with particular individuals. Nothing stops them. But the annual party (perhaps two) brings people together. It is a time for the organization to say thank you; it is a time for networking and catching up; it is a time to recall.

Not everyone looks back with sentimentality and pride. Some of those who do are not inclined to put their hands in their pockets. But many donate with thanks and nostalgia, and all those rose-tinted memories of a lost youth.

So why do businesses not do the same? Why not exploit one's ex-staff as a business opportunity? And why should the idea be restricted to the private sector? Why not hospitals and health centers? Why not councils and civil servants?

Of course, some have woken up to this idea. Many big consultancy firms have long cherished their alumni. In fact, they act like, because they are, postgraduate-oriented universities. They offer websites and newsletters. They effectively do *Friends Reunited* for free. For the small cost of listening to a 15-minute presentation about 'new developments,' which is little more than an upbeat advertorial, old boys and girls can enjoy free soda, nice canapés, a good gossip and an excellent pre-dinner catch-up.

These business organizations want good will not money. They want influential friends of former employees to be interested and impressed. The idea is not a new one. For many years some big stores have had a simple but enjoyable Christmas lunch for ex-employees. The humblest sales staff to the ex-directors, like walk-ons from *Are You Being Served*, claim really to enjoy these events.

Good will does not come cheap. And poisonous bile can be very costly. We know from the studies of what is called business recovery that, paradoxically perhaps, when organizations mess up (overbook, overcharge, etc.) they can recover the situation and make people even happier than had the event not occurred in the first place. Dissatisfied customers can turn into apostles, but also terrorists.

And so it is in organizations. The way people are treated before, on, and after leaving can profoundly influence what they try to do to the organization afterwards. Those who remain also notice that treatment. They know their turn will eventually come: like death and taxes, it is a sure certainty.

Treat someone badly—humiliate them by denying access to the building and giving them three hours and two black bags to clear their desk and leave—and you certainly get more than one highly disenchanted staff member.

Everyone wants to leave with dignity and with thanks. They like to have their contribution acknowledged and they like to think that they will be warmly remembered. And most don't want to close the book with finality. They no doubt have friends and acquaintances left behind. After all, a major source of everybody's friends are people at work.

So why not start an organization alumnus club? Call it whatever suits the ethos of the organization. Plan a couple of events a year and subsidize them. Keep people in contact with one another. Invite them to see the new facilities. Recall the 'good old days.' It is a very wise investment of time and effort.

Business placebo

Placebo: the curse of medical researchers but the friend of evidence-free therapy? Most people think of placebos as 'sugar pills': inert, harmless concoctions that are know to have no curative properties. But we know that, when told (by handsome, omniscient doctors) they contain new miracle drugs, people do (apparently, allegedly) get better. Placebos have persuasiveness not biochemical power.

But there is placebo surgery (people are cut and sewn up again), and placebo pills, injections, plasters, bandages, and placebo therapy.

It has been argued that a lot of people are attracted to alternative medicine, which they testify (in all honesty and seriousness) does help (cure) them, because of the nature of the consultations. Compared to the seven to nine minutes allotted to the patient for a standard consultation at their local doctor's surgery, alternative consultations take much longer, probably involve touch, discussing one's broad life circumstances, and look at emotional as much as physical issues.

Good doctors of all specialties know about and use the placebo effect. Clinical psychologists and psychotherapists know about the therapeutic alliance which means that, whatever type of therapy people have, they seem to get better. They get better because they have the support of an ally or a helper. They are encouraged to face and solve their problems. They set targets and goals. The curious thing is this: the therapist may be radically different in training and therapeutic technique but the effects are the same. Thus the unconscious-mining Freudian therapy, the thought-examining cognitive behavior therapy, and the uncommitted non-directive Rogerian therapy all have much the same effect. And this, despite the fact that they have massive, 100-year-long intellectual fights, a very different training history, and variable ideas about diagnosis, prognosis and therapy.

So what has all this to do with business? Well maybe exactly the same issues apply. Management 'science' also has its ideological division, its specialist practitioners, its preferred ways of functioning. Deming and Drucker disagree. Peters disagrees with himself every few years. Goleman et al. don't overlap much.

And every fad has its residue of practitioners, happily carrying out their step-by-step procedures according to the theoretical manual. So we've had 'quality circles,' and 'management-by-walking-about,' and 'performance management systems.' We once had 'T-groups' and 'management by objectives.'

The new growth industry is business coaching. Is the business coach a counselor, a confessor or a clinician? Or are they teacher, trainer or therapist? Are they simply a management trophy or do they do good work?

The same might even apply to business education—the sacred and fiercely expensive MBA. An MBA is a huge investment. The opportunity costs in middle age are excessive. But the rewards are high. Yet it does not seem to matter terribly much *where* one goes, *what* is taught, and *how* one is examined.

One academic once remarked that, when presenting ideas, any model will do. Despite the fact that some are simple, others complex, some static, others dynamic, some general, others specific, it does not matter which is chosen. They may be contradicting, ideologically opposed, empirically supported or not. It just does not matter.

Placebo theory works like this. When people are coached, trained, or taught they go through various processes. Often this begins with contracting responsibilities. One meets others and hears their experiences. One tries out new skills and ideas in a safe and supportive environment. One has to confront fears, phobias, and frailties head on.

It is a time-out experience to reflect and re-examine. The tyranny of the urgent email and the business meeting seem less important. One's teacher-trainer/coach pays full attention to one. They seem to want to help one really develop one's potential. And this means honestly confronting areas of ignorance, anxiety, and underdevelopment that most senior people have been able to cover up. They help set achievable and important goals and keep the persona on track.

So does it matter what the method is called? It probably does matter how much it costs. But it's an active human placebo. It makes people feel more confident, more in control, more stress-free.

Business self-help

Over the last 20 years book stores have groaned under the weight of a new category of book unknown 25 years ago: the self-help book. The self-help section is bursting with quirky titles, all offering the same hope: read the book and health, happiness, even wealth will be yours.

They are aimed at the naive, the troubled, and the insecure. It has recently been suggested that all these books fall into two essential categories: the victim book and the empowerment book. The victim book does not so much teach as explain. It provides a long list of what psychologists call 'bad objects' to explain why you are unfulfilled and unsuccessful in life and at work. Everything from bad genes, bad parents, and bad bosses, to the class system and international capitalism has been the cause of your plight.

The victim book offers little in the way of help, save perhaps that other old favorite: litigation. But it does focus outward in the belief that other-blame is better than self-blame.

The alternative to the victim book is the empowerment book. This offers hope and is therefore currently much more popular. But most do not suggest a range of skills you might care to, or indeed need to, acquire. Nor do they offer a sort of cognitive behavior therapy or belief system retraining. Most believe it is simply all about 'self' words, like self-belief, self-concept, and self-worth. Make people *feel* good and they will *do* good. Hence the rise and further rise of the self-esteem movement.

Recently, academics have recanted on self-esteem theory, showing there is no evidence for the belief that self-esteem is the key, causal factor in work and life success. Indeed there is much more evidence that success leads to self-esteem, not the other way around. So the treatment for low self-esteem is to give people the knowledge and skills that lead to better relationships and greater productivity, which in turn leads to fulfillment.

Many business books are also self-help books, in the sense that they are meant to be useful, non-technical, and inspirational. However, they come—as one might expect—in rather different categories, as outlined below.

The metaphor/parable

These are very short books about mice and cheese, throwing fish, and the like. They are like parables as they encourage readers to put their own 'spin' on the story in order to identify with it. Some, rather mysteriously, sell in their millions. Their success seems more a consequence of author, guru, and publisher hype than genuine usefulness.

The heroic biography

These are often hagiographies and, one suspects, actually commissioned by the subject of the biography. They are nearly always the story of rags to riches, of blood, sweat, and tears, of (big) triumph and (small, overcome) disaster. They inspire by example. They show how risk-taking, courage, and intuition (but never luck) led the subject to the pinnacle of his (yes always *his*) career.

The seven secret wassanames

People like lists in business. Plus or minus seven. Ten, as in the commandments, is OK but at the limit of business brain capacity. Books like these list essential ingredients to business success. The rank order of points rarely seems important and some look pretty much like one another. But each must be lavishly embellished by examples, stories, and anecdotes.

Magic/silver bullet solutions

This is the one-technique book. It would like us to believe that adopting one (pretty self-evident) process is the key to everything. Re-engineering or EQ, quality circles or performance management system. The story is simple. Use this technique for everything, everywhere, all the time, and all will be (for ever) well.

Schmaltz and sentimentality

The final business self-help book may be more adopted by business people than written for them. It is the Disney of the business book world. It often tells an archetypal story of conquest, or quest. It celebrates all those non-business-like virtues of gratitude, trust, and forgiveness.

There are, however, some useful business books that fall outside these categories. Based on dispassionate, objective academic research, yet related to the author's real-world business consulting experience. Carefully written, yet amusing, with properly referenced sources for further reading. Written by an academic with journalistic tendencies. One author in particular comes to mind, but then modesty forbids …

Chronic email disorder

Seldom does a communication medium have the rapid and all-powerful appeal and effect of email. You can communicate with other people synchronously on the other side of the world for practically nothing. Fast. Cheap. Efficient.

But email has led to many problems. Most people rant on about spam, cc-ing, trivia, and the sheer demands on their time of answering 'correspondence' on a daily basis. Many employees—of all ranks in the organization—claim to spend as much as two hours a day responding to items in their perpetually expanding in-box.

Yet if their email is 'down,' for whatever reason, people experience near panic attacks. Being incommunicado is terrifying. You might be missing crucially important, vital communication. Lost opportunities, lost income, lost gossip. Hence the love/hate relationship with email. The problems of email can be neatly divided into two categories: volume and interpretation.

The volume problem is obvious to all. Despite spam detectors and other filtering devices, most users complain about the sheer volume of messages they receive. A simple, obvious problem is that it is initially very difficult to differentiate the important from the unimportant. There is no obvious or easy filter, no mechanism to prioritize.

How much of business email is important? Some reckon 70 percent of correspondence is gossip of one sort or another and 10 percent cc-ing to keep in the loop. So it's the old 80:20 rule again. The trouble is that email is so efficient. So many people rely on it as a primary method of communication. Your boss, best clients, spouse, and children communicate this way.

Some organizations have decided to bite the bullet. Faced, paradoxically, by reduced efficiency because staff spend all their day sending and receiving email, they have tried to devise new rules. Rules that are offensive and defensive. But rules that are aimed at doing a bit of filtering and helping with prioritizing. Consider the following statements.

- No one is allowed to email people on the same floor or in the same building.
- Chevrons indicating urgency are to be used regularly but sparingly; not more than one 'triple' very urgent in one day.
- No one is not allowed to send more than ten emails per day.
- Cc-ing is allowed only once per day and never to more than seven people.
- No email may contain fewer than 20 words or more than 150, and while bullet points are encouraged, seven is the maximum number.
- If an email is not responded to within 48 hours it should be deleted.
- While on vacation or out of the office, auto-responses should be set up so that senders are aware of your absence.

The above seven, seemingly draconian, rules should be communicated to all staff within the organization and to those in other 'slacker' organizations, so they understand what is happening.

The second problem is tone. Without face-to-face voice tone, it is often easy to misinterpret emails. Doing all that very primitive colon, dash, and bracket emotional encoding (such as :-) or :-!) helps precious little. Capitals are seen as shouting, spelling or typing errors as carelessness or ignorance.

It is often those with low emotional intelligence and social skills that choose to communicate via email. They think it is easier. It isn't. It's harder to read the hidden agenda in emails. Some of the advice given to people when receiving traditional letters may apply.

- Never reply immediately if the email causes strong (negative) emotions. You don't have to sleep on it, but give it a few hours.
- Beware forwarding emails that contain jokes, asides, or personal comments, which can be very contextual.
- Re-read your responses, particularly to emotionally charged emails, at least once.
- Realize that not all emails get delivered.

Email etiquette and advice seems to be needed in the modern office. The email is a powerful device for communication. Busy senior executives can be hounded, bothered, and exasperated by requests, demands, and insults from 'little people' everywhere. But, worse, email addiction may reduce efficiency in an organization.

So why not try the above rules, just for a week or two? If they don't work so be it. But we need to start somewhere. And soon.

Compulsive buying

There are economic, psychological, and obvious utilitarian benefits to most consumer purchases. We need food and clothes, and means of transport, and white goods, and the lot. But nowadays more and more products are sold not on their technical features, but rather their psychological benefits. It's all about identity, image, and values. And that means people can rely on, even be addicted to, specific forms of consumerism, because they offer a sort of psychological crutch. Retail therapy indeed.

There are, quite clearly, the consumption-obsessed: call them addictive or compulsive buyers, must-have fashion victims, or vulgar acquisitive materialists. They are easily recognizable by their (in this order) excessive, uncontrolled, and often impulsive buying of many kinds of products they may never wear or use. They are as preoccupied with shopping as alcoholics are with the next drink. They seem compelled to go to all sales, and spend hours on the web or in stores.

So who are these people? Why do they do it? How many of them are there? They come from all social backgrounds, but the vast majority of them are women. And there are lots and lots of them. We are a highly materialist, consumer-driven society. It's easy to spend, there is much to buy. Advertisements are ubiquitous.

And advertisements for product after product show us that 'to have is to be.' You are what you eat, wear, and drive. Material goods are fashion statements and value statements. Possessions are a way of reinventing yourself, of compensating for faults, even of regulating emotions. They can replace a sense of emptiness, they can even substitute for a relationship.

And goods can be a political statement. Just as shunning certain products and proudly/defiantly showing off others can literally be a political badge, so there is a code for the materially minded. Labels count. Labels shout.

Researchers in this area believe two factors lead to compulsive shopping. Helga Dittmar of Sussex University suggests the two factors that are important. The first she describes as self-discrepancy; this is, in effect, the difference between your perceived actual self and your desired ideal or possible self. The discrepancy idea has been implicated in alcohol abuse, eating disorders, and sexual promiscuity.

The theory is that possessions fill the gap: they reduce the discrepancy; they offer compensation or repair. That is why certain goods seem to appear high on the must-have list for problematic shoppers (clothes, body care, shoes, electrical and leisure goods).

The second is good old-fashioned material values. Materialists believe that possessions are the key to self-definition and happiness. They are an indicator of success and hence a major life goal. Non- or post-materialist values would offer quite different suggestions as to how to deal with these problems.

Studies have shown that problem shoppers are motivated in part by an attempt to change their mood and to improve their self-image as much as to obtain useful goods at good value. Buying does improve their self-image and self-evaluation, but the effect soon wears off. Hence the need to carry on. Hence its addictive nature. And these shoppers do suffer regret. The buying process is deeply psychologically motivated and meaningful.

A comparison of the compulsive and the ordinary non-addicted consumer reveals striking differences. The non-addicted place value and use as primary motives, while for the addicted mood-changing is top priority. The addicted place product uniqueness and status much higher up the pecking order than do non-addicted consumers.

All studies point to strong sex differences. Females iden-tity-repair through shopping much more than men. The male form may manifest itself in the hoarding of very expensive items or frequent indulgence in competitive auctions.

So how to deal with the disorder: pills, debt, counseling, money management? Or good old-fashioned psychotherapy to deal with the image problem, which is part of the real cause. But only part. One can try to reduce materialistic values. All studies of happiness point to the futility of mate-rial goods. People need purpose and meaning in life, good friends, and an opportunity to explore talents. So a week or two helping others in the developing world, alongside other eager enthusiasts, may be just the ticket.

Consumer profiling

Know your consumer. Understand the values, motives, and needs of your consumers, and you, as well as they, might become kings. Get beneath their skin: *really* understand them.

There are many ways to segment markets: geographically, demographically, economically, but why not psychologically? Psychographics started in the 1930s but was developed further in the 1960s; it was an attempt to capture what was going on in consumers' minds when they went shopping or sat responding to media ads. It focused on individuals' preferred activities, interests, opinions, and values in order to gain an understanding of their lifestyles.

Psychographics seeks to describe the motives, needs, and self-concepts of consumers, which have a direct bearing on their responses to products, packaging, advertising, even public relations efforts. The essential idea was to split the market into definable types, which had different preferences and perceptions.

Psychological consumer profiling has two approaches: the general and the specific. The general is an attempt to 'categorize' the population into known, distinct, lifestyle groups. One American system (Values and Lifestyles, 'VALS'), which has been imported and adapted by many countries, has nine categories of consumers, grouped into need-driven, inner-driven, and outer-driven. Some categories—'Survivors' and 'Sustainers'—are at the lower rungs of society. The system distinguishes between Belongers (who fit in rather than stand out), Emulators (who try to make it big), and Achievers (competent, successful, and hard-working).

But do these different groups consume differently?

Indeed. Their consumption of products (i.e. imported wine, cereal), the media (comedy, sport) and participating in activities (fishing, museum visits) is closely related to their types.

This categorization has been revised and updated over time. It has also been challenged by new and improved systems with new questionnaires and fancy labels. The French, of course, have their own unique categorizing system.

In addition to general systems, many manufacturers and advertising specialists have tried to come up with product-specific psychological segmentation. Thus one manufacturer of prescription drugs found four groups: Realists, Authority Seekers, Skeptics, and Hypochondriacs.

Some have attempted segmentation of larger consumer groups. Thus one study conducted many years ago suggested that American women could be classified into Outgoing Optimists, Conscientiousness Vigilants, Apathetic Indifferents, Self-indulgents, Contented Cows, and Worriers, all based on their values and lifestyles. Another study, of the elderly, found distinct groups such as Explorers, Adapters, Pragmatists, Attainers, Martyrs, and Preservers.

Television audiences, supermarket customers, and those after luxury or specialist products such as cars and cameras, have all been the target of enthusiastic profiling gurus. Early studies by companies were aimed at differentiation. What are the peculiar characteristics of people who choose this camera or car, and are they different from those who choose another brand? Do they see themselves differently? Do they use the product differently? All this encourages businesses to target the customer more closely.

A powerful tool to understand markets and inform consumers, or yet another daft misapplication of psychology? Critics make a number of points. First, the so-called unique groups overlap too much. Next, different studies and systems lead to different groupings—it's more a case of imaginative labeling than marketing science. Third, do these profiles add anything to what the shrewd and perceptive marketing person already knows? And is it not just another gimmick?

Well, if it is a gimmick it has stood the test of time. Perhaps as a species we have been taught to think in categories and differentiate between groups. Journalists and lay people make classifications all the time. Frequently, a hated out-group is lambasted in psychographic terminology: 'tree-hugging, muesli-eating, pinko-greenies,' or 'selfish, planet-destroying, greed-is-good merchants.'

It is true—there are patterns to people's values, beliefs, and purchases.

Control at work

The list of job stressors seems to increase over the years, partly as a function of stress research and partly as a function of the stress industry. Boring and repetitive jobs are stressful. Jobs with too heavy a workload are stressful. Jobs with mean colleagues, manipulative supervisors, and Machiavellian managers are stressful. Jobs with poor equipment or unfair payment are stressful. Jobs in organizations shot through with rivalry, distrust, and conflict are stressful.

And, yes, stress has an adverse impact on an individual's physical health and mental well-being. But it can also have a major impact on morale and productivity. Absenteeism, accidents, and walk-outs have all been linked to stress at work.

A manager reading the literature can be forgiven for feeling overwhelmed. So for those seeking parsimony, control-demand theory goes a long way to help both describe the cause and prescribe the answer.

All jobs have demands: things that have to be done. They may have to be done very fast or very slowly; to a very high degree; in a limited space of time; to satisfy the caprice of customers. Demands can be put on many continua, but most of us know the essential difference between a high- or low-demand job.

Some jobs, by their nature, cannot be changed much. Jobs like journalism and catering will always be time pressured. Others, like being a teacher or social worker, will always involve difficult people.

But it is the other side of the equation that offers more hope and more interest. This is the individual's perception of the degree of control they have at work. Some jobs allow massive employee discretion or decision latitude. Some people can decide when and where to work, how their various tasks are performed, even to what standard.

Self-employed people, those in some educational and research institutes and those in some high level jobs have a good deal of personal control at work. At the other extreme is the Charlie Chaplin *Modern Times* machine-paced worker, who is merely a cog (almost literally) in the great process. The process dictates everything: the employee has virtually no say, no control, no options.

And, of course, there is a difference between real control and perceived control. The former is objective, the latter subjective. Thus a crowded office, or lift, or room can be defined by the number of people per square meter (objective), or how crowded people feel sitting in their Dilbert cubicles or at their terminals. The degree of control felt differs from individual to individual.

It's pretty easy to measure perceived control. It varies quite widely between employees in the same job and it has many consequences. In one study of nurses, their objective and subjective workload was measured. Perceived control was linked to the latter, not the former. And many, many studies have related perceived control to self-reported stress and physical illness.

What is more interesting about control is that it helps to buffer the adverse effects of high demands. It has been established that high-demand jobs lead to adverse reactions, particularly among those with low perceived control. Those with higher control see and treat the same demands as challenges to be overcome rather than threats.

To have some control over aspects of the work task is usually helpful but, of course, it must be relevant to the stressful situation itself. Control affects emotional reactions to events because it minimizes the maximum damage that can occur. And control leads to better coping.

Those who feel they have no control or have lost control

may and do adopt destructive behaviors toward themselves (e.g. excessive drinking), their colleagues, their equipment, their customers, or any external feature of the organization. They may do this in an overt or passive-aggressive way.

All people at work seem motivated to exercise some control over their working style and environment. Hence the enthusiasm for options such as flexi-time, work–life balance options, shift swapping, and working from home. The empowerment movement was all about control, too. It tried to give more decision-making power to certain, often traditionally powerless, groups in the workplace.

Indeed people downsize, trading money and prestige for control. Perhaps that explains why the happiest people are craftsmen and artisans who work at their own speed, in their own studios, to produce things that are an index of their taste, skill, and passion.

Cults and mind control

Why do people join the Masons, the Rotarians or a political party? Because of what they offer: friendship, connections, identity, an opportunity to make a contribution. Are the motives the same as joining the Order of the Solar Temple, the Branch Davidians, the Taliban, Hamas, or al-Qaeda? How are acceptable social groups and organizations different from (dangerous) cults?

There is a great deal of interest in 'cults,' which can take many forms: they may be religious or racial, political or mystical, self-help or pseudo-psychological, but they all have half a dozen recognizable characteristics.

◆ Powerful and exclusive dedication/devotion to an explicit person or creed.
◆ Use of 'thought-reform' programs to integrate, socialize, persuade, and therefore control members.
◆ A well-thought-through recruitment, selection, and socialization process.
◆ Attempts to maintain psychological and physical dependency among cult members.
◆ An insistence on reprogramming the way people see the world.
◆ Consistent exploitation of group members specifically to advance the leader's goals.

Cults nearly always go in for milieu control signals: a different, unfamiliar setting with different rules, terms, and behavior patterns. Ultimately, psychological and physical harm (or threats of this) can be used to control cult members, their friends and relatives, and possibly the community as a whole.

Most cults start their induction by trying to stop both individualistic and critical thinking; like the army, their job is first to break you then remake you in their own image. This involves the introduction of a 'sacred creed' that members may have to live by. Through open confession and subordination of the individual to the doctrine, the cult ensures control and 'purity.' Cults deliberately induce powerful emotions like fear and guilt, but also pride. They tend to develop their own language, dress, and signals, which demonstrate their 'specialness.'

But the central question is whether organizations usually thought of as good and legitimate do things differently than cults. Do the Boy Scouts or Rotarians operate psychologically at any level?

All too often, we explain strange, unexpected behavior (like joining a cult) in terms of the dispositions (personality) of others; they (the poor gullible naive indoctrinated members) have quite defective personalities. But we explain more common behavior in terms of the appeal of an accepted group's philosophy, leaders, or benefits. Thus sad inadequates join cults, but altruistic, caring people join the Church.

Applying misunderstood psychiatric labels to those who join extremist groups offers little or no explanation for their behavior. It often represents little more than a moralistic condemnation. Rather than immediately trying to blame extremists for being different, it is equally important to try to understand the psychological appeal of cults, extremist groups and political cells, as well as some business organizations.

Any analysis of the make-up of individuals in cult groups shows surprisingly large diversity in terms of age, career, education, ideology, and talents. They can attract the postgraduate and the illiterate, the teenager and the 'senior citizen,' the solidly middle class, and those on the fringes of society. It is not so much their demography that is important as their psychological needs.

Studies on those who have signed up for all sorts of cults and extremist groups have, however, shown that they do have similar and sophisticated recruitment promises, induction techniques, and social influence agendas. They use methods of 'indoctrination' and 'mind control' no different from all groups, though they are no doubt a lot more intensely applied in some cases. The mind-controlling techniques of extremist groups are little different from those of the army, religious organizations, and prisons. These 'wicked' techniques are in fact well known: demanding total, consistent compliance and conformity, using heavy persuasive techniques, creating dissonance, emotional manipulation. They differ only in intensity and duration … and thus in effectiveness.

What do all groups (cult and non-cult) offer a potential recruit? Answer: friendship, identity, respect, and security. They also offer a world-view: a way of discerning right from wrong, good from bad. These are powerful incentives for all people, whatever their background—we are social animals. But they offer more: a structured lifestyle and the ability to acquire new skills. Through their (very different) ideologies they also offer moral explanations into how the world works. They provide clear answers to difficult and big questions: what it all means, the secret of happiness, life after death, the difference between right and wrong, who is with us and who against us, the saved and the damned.

Even political groups have a sort of religious agenda, and a language of revenge, purification, justice, which is often very 'old testament.' There is usually within most extremist cult groups surprisingly little violence and often a healthy lifestyle, at least in terms of exercise, diet, and so on. And many promise the ability to heal physical and psychological illnesses … even the illness of society as a whole. Many promise the greatest gift of all: immortality.

Essentially five things make extreme groups dangerous to their members.

1. They demand that they sever all ties with people (family, friends) and organizations (schools, churches). This naturally makes them more dependent on the cult itself and helps create the person's new identity. They start again, wipe the slate clean. This rule is also found in extreme in Christian monastic orders.
2. The members are required to show immediate and unquestioning obedience to rules and regulations, which may be arbitrary, petty, or pointless. The idea is to ensure allegiance and obedience. This strategy is used to 'break in' all army recruits. It is the very stuff of boot camps.
3. Group members often have to do long hours of tedious work. It may be drilling, begging for money, or cooking, followed by compulsory reading, chanting, or mediating. Recruits usually become physically, emotionally, and mentally exhausted. Sleep deprivation is a good start. It's all part of the induction process.
4. All groups need money to exist. Some are very much into money both as an end and a means. This may, therefore, quickly involve recruits getting involved in illegal, or semi-legal, activities. Groups that are state supported or those with a long history of operation may, however, be different. Members need to understand how, when, and why money is required, and to set about getting it—quickly.
5. Groups make exit-costs very high. Leaving is associated with failure, persecution, and isolation. It is more than just a waste of time and effort. They make you feel as if nothing will ever be the same as you will be an outcast. It is made to sound a very unattractive, indeed impossible, option.

But is it true that certain individuals are more receptive to the message of cults than other? Recruiters know that what they appear to have in common is they are at some transitional phase in their life: something has gone and not been replaced. They may have moved location, or given up work or education. They may have just left the bosom of the family because of age or poverty or divorce. They may have drifted away from their religion or ideological roots. They are dislodged from their social group ... and looking for another.

In short, they often feel alienated; they experience all the meaninglessness, powerlessness, and helplessness that goes with that state. They can feel increasingly isolated from the commercial, political, and technical world, which seems to offer little to them. Disaffected, often angry and resentful, they can seek each other out.

Enter the group recruiter. They are introduced into a group with simple (but 'sensible') answers. They offer simple rules, a simple lifestyle, and social support. Most are happy to trade off their liberty (and assets such as they are) for the (illusory) glory, power, and security of that group. The group (cult) appears to offer all they need and want.

Rather shy, unassertive people, who seem inhibited and awkward in social situations, are particularly attracted to groups with formulaic interaction patterns, with predictability and rule following.

Extreme groups offer simple, clear messages in an increasingly complex world. Old certainties are crumbling; ethics, even science, is portrayed as having only relative truths. The world is corrupt, evil, unfair, and very complex. So a group or leader that offers a sensible, sane explanation for the complex world, a secure group, and personal salvation is very attractive. They come in many forms: politicians of the extreme left or right, religious leaders, romantic revolutionaries, persuasive writers, power-hungry individuals, brilliant orators, and movie-star saviors.

People who join extreme groups are not strange, disturbed, sheep-like idiots. We are social animals and members of many groups. The more secretive the group the more we are likely to label it a cult. The more zealous the member the more likely we are to call them deviants. And if they are involved in quasi-military activity they are terrorists.

All the above applies to saboteurs or Luddites, if people are group members and act on behalf of groups. A lot of dark-side behavior in organizations is group work. Certain forms of stealing and cheating cannot be done by individuals alone. People club together to avenge themselves. And they do things on behalf of groups that may seem strange and unacceptable primarily because they do not fully comprehend the value of group membership.

No one sees her/himself as a cult member. The word cult is pejorative. Indeed, even members of fairly extreme groups like Trappist monks or Amish farmers would never think of themselves as cult members. But they owe their survival to many of the principles outlined above.

ATTITUDE SURVEYS

Are attitude surveys ever worth the money and effort? It's a pretty big industry, so there will be a lot of people eager to sell a survey's multiple benefits. They bring, we are told, a snapshot of company morale at any one period in time. They show, apparently, which areas management need to concentrate on. They can tell if a change program or an 'M & A' is working.

But there are three important objections to conducting attitude surveys. First, they all yield practically the same results. Second, attitude surveys rarely offer any straightforward and realistic solutions to problems: it is far from clear what to do with the results. Third, attitudes do not predict behavior (the reverse is true), so why bother with epiphenomena.

Call them climate surveys or engagement-trackers or morale monitors—attitude surveys are nearly always a set of statements about various aspects of life within the organization. Questions usually tap into issues such as attitudes to customers and supervision, innovation, or communication. The output is frequently a glossy, multi-colored report with bar graphs and pie charts. And often the results are broken down not by the old favorites of age, sex, and class, but by groupings such as level, specialty, and region.

Consultants may supposedly tailor-make an attitude survey to the particular circumstances of an organization, or they may use a standard survey so as to benchmark this particular organization. Most prefer this form because, well, you make more money that way. You can run expensive focus groups for garrulous work shirkers; you can interview and ingratiate senior managers; you can try harder to embed yourself in the organization. And after x days you can create the unique, tailor-made 'Acme Widget' staff survey that taps into all the crucial attitudes that shape the behavior of key staff.

The first problem is that it is possible to predict the results long before putting the survey on the intranet. There is always a 'communication' problem. People complain that they do not get told what they need to know. This despite avalanches of cc-ed emails, internal communication posters, magazines and newspapers, weekly meetings, and the like.

Surveys always show that staff don't get enough information. They don't say what they want to know, who should give it to them, or how they are best informed. There seems to be a generalized belief that senior staff have a library of important secrets that they are not willing to share with their staff. A conspiracy of silence? Paranoia? Perhaps.

Worse, the staff survey can give contradictory results. Staff are, at one and the same time, overloaded with information but starved of it. They are swamped by trivia and starved of secrets. But no obvious solution is offered by the staff, so managers end up being frustrated.

The second predictable feature is pay disenchantment. Ask people about their 'comp and ben' and they appear universally pissed off. Are they fairly and equitably paid? Are they paid well according to market rates? 'NO!'—they are all under-benefited. They give more than they get; they have done so for years. All their friends in comparable professions are paid more. They are badly paid. This result is so predictable and infuriating that those who commission the research choose not to ask the question. They often know about market rates and can demonstrate that staff are wrong. Their approach is not to encourage whinging. Further, they know, sometimes from previous experience, that increasing salaries and perks, or whatever, has no effect on the answers to these attitude questions.

Third, if you ask about morale you always get the same result. People believe three things about morale in the organization. They think that morale across the organization is on a clear, remorseless decline, and has been for some time. They also believe that things are OK in their small area, in their section. Their morale has held up, but it is bad elsewhere.

They also experience stress, poor work–life balance, and demands to do more work in less time to higher standards.

Attitudinal results rarely make fascinating reading. Ask the client to predict the results before the survey and many are so accurate you wonder why they commissioned the (expensive) study in the first place. But, worse than that, the results rarely even hint at what actions might be taken to change those attitudes. They do not explain how to make the workplace happier, more productive, more pleasant.

Attitude surveys describe attitudes. But they do not indicate what causes them or, more importantly, causes them to change. Should we worry, though? Aren't attitudes almost epiphenomenal? There has been a debate in psychology since the First World War on whether, how, when, and why attitudes predict behavior. If the causal path is *from* attitudes *to* behavior then changing attitudes leads to changing behavior. But if the causal nexus is the opposite, it makes attitudes far less interesting and important—change behavior and you change attitudes.

The data is in, the jury are back: we know the answer. And it is the latter. In the UK, for example, there were ads that 'encouraged' people to use their car's seatbelts. Many people, despite all the expert advice given, and all that palaver, ignored the ads. Then the law was changed, making the wearing of seatbelts compulsory: it changed behavior and has changed attitudes.

One recent study looked at the attitude–behavior debate in terms of the job satisfaction–productivity link. Are happy people productive, or does productivity bring happiness? Should you try to design workplaces that maximize productive behaviors, or should you spend your bucks making staff as happy as possible? It's difficult research and has to be done longitudinally (over time) to sort out cause and effect. The results from many studies gave the answer published in the prestigious *Journal of Applied Psychology*. Make sure, through management training and appropriate processes, that it is easy for people to maximize their productivity. The reward of productivity is, of course, intrinsic and extrinsic, and this leads to satisfaction. Productive workers reap the rewards of their output—one of which is old-fashioned cash.

Spending time and effort trying to raise job satisfaction is much less successful. Satisfaction is more clearly a result than a cause of productivity.

So what's the point of spending a lot of money on attitude surveys? We know what the answers will be and we know we will not find achievable ideas. We also know that attitudes are affected by behavior, and not vice versa. So we should save the company's cash and make it easier for people to achieve their targets and be really productive.

Deluded dimwits, demure dunces

Both for reasons of political correctness and educational faddism most adults have not taken a proper, validated intelligence test. They may have tried their hand at crosswords and Sudoku. They may be aware that they can still do 'mental arithmetic' faster than their friends. But do they really know how bright they are?

Intelligence tests go back years. The most celebrated usually involved between 8 and 14 subtests of everything from vocabulary and general knowledge to memorizing strings of numbers and arranging patterns. They are among the most robust of all psychometric tests and the single best predictor of success in educational and work contexts.

Most of us receive feedback on our abilities, but television shows such as *American Idol* have demonstrated, very clearly, how deluded people can be. They treat the contest, as one judge put it, as an 'attitude not aptitude test.' Perhaps they have been encouraged by doting relatives, perhaps they have sought or recalled only positive feedback, but many certainly have an idiosyncratically odd and deluded perception of their own talent.

With respect to intelligence there are quite simply three groups of individuals. The first are self-aware: they know how bright they are. This may result not from test feedback but from good education, astute observation, and clear self-insight into their cognitive abilities. The bright, the average, and the less talented know who they are. They know what others can do and most lead their life accordingly. Of course, success in life—at work, in relationships, and in the pursuit of happiness—is not solely dependent on intelligence. Personality, good health, supportive friends, and a robust belief system can all contribute significantly to life success.

But if there are self-aware people with a good grasp of their aptitude there are two other groups less attuned to their actual abilities. And they are characterized by inappropriate modesty or humility and excessive self-aggrandizement or hubris.

The second, the humble and meek—who shall inherit the earth—appear to believe they are not particularly cognitively talented. Not necessarily a sausage short of a fry-up or a coupon short of a toaster, but much less able than they actually are. Certain cultures, in an attempt to dissuade unacceptable signs of arrogance, hubris, or intellectual superciliousness, particularly in the female of the species, encourage this attitude. They are taught not to boast, show off, or exhibit intelligence.

Being bright but unaware could, however, bring costs to the individual and indeed wider society, not so much in what they do but in what they don't do. They seem born to 'waste their fragrance on the desert air,' to underachieve, never to realize their full potential.

Thus humility should not be confused with self-deprecation, which is often the very opposite. The idea of the English understatement, for instance, is to put others off their guard, to reduce envy, or to make opponents underestimate you.

The third category seems to be the most common. These are the beneficiaries (or victims) of too much self-esteem therapy. They have no weaknesses, only 'developmental opportunities', and no failures, only delayed successes. They believe with either zero or twisted evidence that they are considerably brighter than they are. They tend to be neither analytic, curious, nor quick on the uptake. They are imaginative only in the sense that they imagine levels of ability they don't have.

Not all have hubris, but some do and it's often very unattractive. However, it also has some benefits. It gives confidence, which is a very attractive social asset. Most people assume their confidence is a function of their experience and feedback. Thus if you are super-confident of your cognitive ability or academic prowess, it is because you know you can learn things easily, solve problems, have encyclopedic knowledge. People give you the benefit of the doubt … and the individuals in this category exploit it.

So what are the drawbacks? The answer to this is revealed when people have to perform real tasks and receive clear, unambiguous, and unbiased feedback. It is then that hubris turns to fury, disbelief, and depression. It has been said that the rise in adolescent suicides in some countries is mainly due to backfiring self-esteem therapy.

It's always better to try to work within the natural constraints of your natural gifts.

Demons, drivers, and defenses

The most unlikely individuals elect either to have or to avoid psychotherapy. For most people the question of why visit a practitioner of the 'talking cure' is hardly worth asking. It's like the issue of visiting the doctor.

But precisely why do people visit the doctor? For advice, sympathy, a diagnosis, relief from pain, reassurance? They go both to prevent illness and to restore health. Some go more often than others. Some go more than they should and some less, according to doctors.

And many medics will tell you that patients present with as many psychological as physical issues. Some tell you that three-quarters of their patients really need a clinical psychologist or a social worker, not a doctor.

But there is still a taboo around visiting psychologists and psychiatrists. While it is not unusual to hear the old-fashioned, almost-boast, 'I am under the doctor,' it is extremely rare, save perhaps in New York or California, to hear 'I lie on Dr. Ruth's couch!'

It's less unacceptable than it used to be but it is still rare to hear people describe their motives for, or experiences of, psychotherapy. Drug abuse and addiction, depression, and phobia are talked and written about. And some celebrities are happy to 'come out' as grateful recipients of psychotherapy … be it alone or in groups.

But others are afraid of therapy. They are afraid, not of the shame and embarrassment that may result from all the self-disclosure—they are frightened it could, in a way, destroy part of their essential being. The problem is that, in seeking to discover and destroy demons, one has to break defenses and hence demobilize powerful drivers.

Most of us know people who are driven. They may be driven by wealth or power or the need to achieve. All but the least insightful know they are driven. But most do not know why. They may be driven by childhood fears and memories of being rejected, powerless, or simply being unpopular. They may be driven by a sense of physical inferiority.

Some may still, even in late middle age, be trying to please a long-dead parent. Or they may still be metaphorically competing with peers or siblings in the playground. Hence the small bullied child learns to be a comic; the stutterer a public speaker; the bright boy from a poor background a multi-millionaire. It does not always have to be compensatory. And it does not have to lead to misery.

But drivers are unconscious; certainly below self-awareness. It is easier for observers, friends, and family to understand and articulate the nature, perhaps even the cause, of their drives.

One reason for the inaccessibility of the drivers are the defenses we build. It was Anna Freud, daughter of that old Moravian sex addict, who listed the typical ego mechanisms of defense such as repression, regression, projection, and reaction formation.

The idea is that, over time, we learn to protect our fragile ego—the self. We develop defenses for all sorts of reasons. They are our protective shields. Some are more primitive than others; some more acceptable; some more efficient.

But therapy is often aimed at reconstruction. And to reconstruct one first needs to break down, to destroy and, in the case of individuals, to make very vulnerable. Some therapists chip away at the defenses, not to destroy the ego but to explore it … and put it together again so as to be more resilient, more healthy, more adaptable.

Sometimes those who know someone in therapy report quite dramatic changes in their acquaintance. They may seem to lose their sense, or at least use of, humor. They may seem a lot less frenetic. They may seem less pensive, more contented. A bit of dynamism might go. Energy is lost. The life force seems some how reduced. And this is the fear for those going into therapy. Writers and painters, novelists and musicians are worried that their springs of inspiration might dry up. Often with special talents they can channel their pain and fear, as well as passion and joy into their art. They often know how to harness the power of their demons.

But if the demons cause too much pain and doubt they paralyze rather than inspire. The important thing, of course, is balance. Indeed, we know the extreme highs and lows suffered by manic-depressive or bipolar people supply the creatively talented with wonderful material for their novels, poetry, and art. Yet there is often great cost to this roller-coaster riding.

For some creatives the pain is worth the gain. They do not fully, even partially, understand the source and process of their particular inspiration and energy. And they rightly fear that exploring it might change or reduce it.

Many, but not all, individuals who seek therapy know the risks, akin to the side effects of conventional medicine, and accept them.

Depressive realism

What do Peter Pan, Pollyanna, and positive psychology have in common? One answer is that they accentuate the positive; they look on the bright side of life.

There are whole industries dedicated to perpetuating the positive aspects of human existence. Most movies end in victory. The world is just; people are good (really); virtues are rewarded.

The self-esteem industry also does the positive thing. It asserts, with complete and charming lack of evidence, that positive self-esteem drives success. Not the other way around. Feel good about yourself and you succeed in life, so there are counselors and trainers and teachers who try to instill, sometimes in the most unlikely person, a sense of positivity.

There is, furthermore, a massive army of teachers trained to deal with that curious cancer-like malady of our times, namely depression. The gloom of ever present sadness haunts many people. The slough of despond is both draining and unhealthy.

But nearly 20 years ago psychoanalysts made a counterintuitive discovery. It was that in a number of quite different situations depressed people are more realistic and accurate in their perceptions than non-depressed people. It led to the disputed concept of 'depressive realism.'

The experiments conducted by the psychologists involved depressed and non-depressed people making judgments about personal control. Where they had little control over the outcome of an event, the depressed realized this sooner than the over-optimistic non-depressed.

The fact that depressed people were more accurate in

assessing control contradicted the idea that depression is partly caused and maintained by problems in the brain concerning attention, processing of information, or memory retention. As a result of these difficulties people become and stay depressed because they are supersensitive to negativity and relatively blind to positivity. They notice and remember the bad things. When these people fail they never forget; when they succeed they never remember.

Certainly the dispute is far from resolved and experiments have shown contradictory results. Some recent studies suggest that the depressed individual does not process information about contexts well, which leads to the depressive realism effect. Clinicians seem very eager to dispel the possibility that depressive individuals have a better take on the world.

Soon the world divided neatly into two camps. The first argued that depressed individuals perceive the world and all that is in it, particularly themselves, with a strong, unwarranted and unflattering negativity bias. They are the merchants of gloom, Job's comforters, carriers of negativity. They dwell in the darkness and carry no light. But more critically they are wrong and biased. They see the glass half empty *when it is not*. They see, remember, and remark on the bad things about themselves. And therefore they need help. They need reality therapy. They need help to see the truth, beauty, and goodness in the world.

The opposing side argues for depressed realism; this is the idea that it is the optimists who are biased. Life is grim and life is earnest. We live in a random world and have to resign ourselves to fatalism. It is the vision of Hobbes, not Rousseau. People are coy, capricious, irascible. They are egocentric, lazy and, for the most part, disagreeable. Life is indeed nasty, brutish, and short. Sticks work better than carrots.

There is, particularly to the British ear, nothing quite as schmaltzy, fake and annoying as those Disneyesque merchants of bland, naive optimism. The Rousseauian myth of kind, hard-working, empathic individuals, who only have to be liberated from their chains of bad management. Hence all that guff about unleashing and unblocking ability, of firing up the flame of potential.

When the Californian airhead version of reality is peddled by trainers, gurus, and television presenters, the depressive realistic reach for their revolvers. They know it is flim-flam, pie-in-the-sky, non-reality.

But it's no fun being around a 'can't do,' 'we are all doomed' puritan. We all prefer non-bias—neither optimism nor pessimism, just realism. Of course, the postmodernists dispute even the possibility of realism existing: there is no truth, no reality, no objectivity.

Devising new courses

Is training in your organization a reward or a punishment? Do you associate seminars, symposia, and workshops with fun 'networking' in nice country hotels? Or do you remember them as a curious mixture of humiliation, boredom, and being lectured by those with half your experience and education but twice as much arrogance and extravagance?

The training business is certainly a big one. Most hotels, it seems, stay afloat through conferences where hundreds book up the place for a few days to discuss strategy, release their creativity, or master the new magic bullet solution.

Consultants, gurus, and training experts have to come up with new products. Once a new concept—like emotional intelligence, quality circles, or process re-engineering—comes onto the market, the piranhas have a feeding frenzy. Courses are available everywhere. It becomes very difficult to differentiate between them in quality and take-home value.

Organizations are prepared to spend millions on management training. They find it both important and necessary. But few can maintain a sufficiently up-to-date and flexible in-house team to do the job at senior levels. Anyway, no board member is likely to accept training from a member of staff three levels their junior. Hence the training consultants.

The problem lies in updating courses and making them sound new, sexy, and must-have. Some words are 'in' while others soon go out of fashion. Sometimes it is desirable to make the course a little vague.

Consider the wonderful solution given in the table and text that follow.

The computational course categorizer

1.	Behavioral	Action-learning	Advice
2.	Biological	Client-centered	Analysis
3.	Certified	Didactic	Coaching
4.	Complementary	Entrepreneurial	Conference
5.	Confessional	Interpersonal	Contracting
6.	Confrontational	Neo-Freudian/Jungian	Counseling
7.	Emotional	Neurolinguistic	Education
8.	Experiential	Outdoor	Gathering
9.	Experimental	Placebo-controlled	Guidance
10.	Interactional	Rational-emotive	Paradigm
11.	Inspirational	Team-based	Management
12.	Multi-disciplinary	Senior management	Masterclass
13.	Post-millennial	Strategic	Modeling
14.	Preventative	Systems based	Seminar
15.	Scientific	Vocational	Solution
16.	Spiritual	Web-enhanced	Therapy

This is the ideal solution for the imaginative, growing, training company. Choose any three terms: confessional, client-centered, coaching; experiential, rational-emotive, masterclass; post-millennial, systems based, modeling; multi-disciplinary, web enhanced, education.

Sounds great: new, mysterious, and cutting edge. Naturally the course could contain practically anything. And that's the brilliance of the marketing: old stuff can very easily be recycled, updated. No bad thing, necessarily. Each generation has to rediscover some pretty fundamental concepts in its own language. So charm became social skills became emotional intelligence.

Often business people have to be enticed into training. Organizations see training as either a reward or a punishment; rarely a necessity. This is in part due to the fact that it is devilishly difficult to prove that training 'works'—that it has a direct and measurable effect on the bottom line.

Most senior managers avoid training like the plague, not because it is not important or they don't need it, but rather because they fear being 'shown up' in front of talented and thrusting youngsters with twice the talent and energy.

Hence the need for repackaging and reinventing training courses.

Dysfunctional consumer behavior

Shop 'til u drop, retail therapy, and compulsive buying behavior are all recognized as postmodern, but certainly not post-material syndromes.

Stores have replaced the savannah. Increased wealth, leisure, and choice have meant that people spend a great deal of their free time on one form of consumerism or another. It may be the call of the mall, surfing the web, or an exclusive shopping experience.

As a result there are now many known consumer behavior disorders. They include kleptomania and shopping phobia. Psychiatrists do recognize compulsive buying as a disorder, but seem uncertain as to whether it is essentially a compulsive-obsessive, impulse control, or mood disorder.

Perhaps they need a little help. These dozen recognizable syndromes, disorders, and problems appear to occur both in mild forms and extreme versions. They probably are treatable but may be on the increase. Perhaps it is time for a 'shopping tsar.'

Consider the following examples.

Post-traumatic after-sales service withdrawal

This is a frequently occurring malady, marked by promises not being met. Assured that all questions will be answered and all problems fixed after handing over cash for a product, you discover nothing like that occurs.

Delusional bargain impulse

This is the irrational belief that there are real bargains to be found in store basements or at sale times, and that bargains are not just stock that stores can't sell.

Bipolar BOGOF dysfunction

This is almost Tourette's syndrome, associated with the secret belief that BOGOF is a swear word. It is associated with buying two of everything when you need half of one thing.

Habitual closing-down-sale fantasy

Another bargain hunter ploy. 'All must go,' is the cry. And with the gullible indeed it does.

Unconscious celebrity-endorsed complex

This is the belief that celebrities who endorse products really like and use them, as opposed to being paid large fees to make like they do.

Generalized 'brand new and improved' obsession

Not all new is improved, as Coca-Cola found out. This is a desire to be modern, up to date, in the swim. To make a product statement about modernity.

Acute free gift malady

This is vulnerability to the oldest trick in the book: a worthless, gaudy trinket attached to an extremely expensive item to lure in the unwary.

Episodic guarantee fetish

These people come from an earlier time when you did not throw away products simply because you got bored with them. They come from an era where things broke down—hence the need for, and fetish about, time-period guarantees.

Degenerative helpline assisted neurosis

Electronic products become ever more complicated and perplexing, so much so that one has to be talked down by ever present, ever tolerant super-nannies. Some won't buy anything unless the helpline is guaranteed.

Adolescent last chance disorder

This is the 'last day of the sale, get on with it' trick. Interestingly, it works both with ditherers and with impulsives who, on seeing the sign, immediately cough up.

Borderline percent-off psychosis

This problem arises because the purchaser buys according to a meaningless number. So the retailer doubles the price and then offers 50 percent off.

Ethics committees

Many kinds of public institutions have found it necessary to appoint ethics committees. Fads and fashions, political correctness, increased litigation? Or wise practice?

Ethics committees are there usually to facilitate decisions as to whether a course of action—such as conducting a research project—fulfils certain criteria. The theory is that a group of (wise) individuals can perform a disinterested evaluation of a proposed course of action that minimizes harm to any and maximizes benefits to many.

Ethics committees are, then, in some senses like juries. One crucial difference is how people get into these groups. Juries are usually co-opted, conscripted, and many fight kicking and screaming to be exempt. On the other hand, ethics committees are often staffed by happy volunteers eager to take part.

The jury system has come under increasing critical scrutiny, not only for its expense and inefficiency but for its record of poor judgments. But at the same time ethics committees appear to be mushrooming in schools and hospitals, universities, and businesses.

There are three major problems with the way people use and think about ethics committees. The first is around ethics itself. The assumption is that, just as one does not have to have any detailed knowledge or understanding of the law to join a jury, so one need know nothing of ethics to join an ethics committee.

This analogy is wrong for a number of reasons. First, there are competing ethical systems. What is right and just for the situational ethicist is simply not true for the absolutist. Different rules may be seen to apply. Hence ethics. One may have different interpretations of the law, but one legal system.

Next, it is the role of the judge not only to control the court but, when necessary, to explain the law. Judges are experts and highly knowledgeable in the way that the chairperson of a committee is not.

Third, jurors are vetted in the way volunteers for ethical committees are not. Indeed, it has been suggested that the motives for people volunteering for ethics committees are themselves far from ethical.

It would therefore be desirable, perhaps necessary, for someone to know something about ethics and to have a view on what system they intend to follow. Are they utilitarians or not? What principles should be followed?

The second fallacy is that groups of individuals make more considered, cautious, and wise decisions than individuals alone. But in fact there is a wealth of evidence suggesting the opposite—namely that groups nearly always make more extreme decisions. That is, they can be excessively cautious or excessively risk-taking. There are well-documented reasons as to why this may occur.

For ethics committees it is too easy to say no. To default on the negative certainly decreases their chances of being blamed. It is not difficult to find reasons for not doing something. In this sense ethics committees can be extremely conservative and pro the status quo.

The third problem concerns the real reason why we have seen a tremendous increase in the number of ethics committees in the first place. The answer is litigation. Avaricious, lawyer-inspired litigiousness is with us. Ethics committees may or may not help the problem of litigation. Unless, of course, it is their explicit remit and there is a lawyer on board.

To make ethics committees function, the following seem useful requirements. First, have a chair who knows about ethics. Second, decide on a system or code that is to be implemented. Third, choose and vet committee members carefully and do not have too many. Fourth, have a lawyer on board. Fifth, ensure this process and dynamic is functional not dysfunctional. Sixth, ensure the committee knows precisely its function and duties. Seventh, have an appeals procedure. Eighth, ensure people have a set period on the committee and do not automatically renew. Ninth, give the committee feedback on their earlier decisions. Tenth, consider changing the name from ethics committee to something else.

Evaluation

There are many ways to assess or evaluate students. They can sit old-fashioned timed written tests: three to five open-ended questions in two to three hours. They can also perform multiple-choice tests that don't involve writing but, rather, identifying the correct answers.

Or, they can have a short (or indeed long) oral test: a viva voce. PhDs are examined this way. Two examiners might probe a candidate for between two and ten hours.

Then there is continuous assessment in the sense that students hand in various assignments (essays, projects, presentations, posters). While these have deadlines they allow long periods of time for preparation (and, these days, plagiarism).

There are of course interesting variants of all of the above. So there can be an open-book test, which these days may mean access to a laptop, so that less is dependent on memory and more on how to gain access to and evaluate information. Written tests may last for long periods—up to eight hours—so they are less time pressured, and people can leave when they are properly finished. Some are even more radical: students are encouraged to set their own questions and then answer them.

Equally, the oral test could comprise the evaluation of a prepared presentation, or the assessment of an off-the-cuff argument. It is more likely to be a question-and-answer session, but the number of examiners needs to be decided.

Perhaps the hottest question in continuous assessment is whether it should or can be a group effort. A 'consortium' of students may work together on a project and each receive the mark given to the group effort. This begets several issues, such as who determines the group composition (students or teachers?), the maximum and minimum size of the group, whether the process (input of each individual) or only the output is examined.

There are numerous very important questions and consequences arising from the choice of examination method. Which is the fairest? What type of individuals favor one technique over another?

Researchers have found some pretty reliable relationships. Extroverts quite like vivas, while introverts hate them and feel they cannot and do not give their best. Brighter students like the old-fashioned time-pressured written test more than less intelligent students (as determined by IQ tests).

Conscientious, hard-working students prefer individually assessed continuous assessment. Moody and unstable students are ill disposed to any and all evaluation methods. Creative students tend not to like either multiple-choice or group work. Teachers and lecturers often favor multiple-choice and oral tests because these methods require less effort than marking scripts.

The question of fairness is complex. Are oral tests unfair to introverts? Are timed tests unfair to those of a sensitive (neurotic) disposition? Does group-work continuous assessment take any account of freeloaders?

The issue is controversial because it is not always clear what an assessment is meant to evaluate. Is it memory or power of criticism? Is it vocabulary or skill? Is it ability to perform under pressure? Or retrieve, process, and present salient facts? Another concern is assessor reliability—that is, how much agreement there is between different examiners. Most tell you that agreement is highest at the top and the bottom of the performance rankings, but fuzzier in the middle. Many examiners are surprised, many delighted, at their high levels of agreement given the intrinsic subjectivity of the task.

So much for reliability—what about validity? What does an A grade in Mathematics signify? What should you expect of a first-class graduate in Psychology? What does an MSc in Airline Catering mean you can do?

What do tests and vivas and continuous assessment measure? Does continuous assessment measure sustained work activity better than one-off tests? Does group work measure social skills better than multiple-choice tests? Do oral exams measure confidence and bravado rather than knowledge?

Certainly the examination method has 'noise' in the sense that it probably measures things other than those it explicitly sets out to measure. Most examinations attempt to assess critical thinking around a particular knowledge base. The assumption is that candidates have acquired knowledge and skills in a particular area, which they are able to evaluate, summarize, and demonstrate. But this may involve temperament as well as ability.

Hence the harder, more salient question. Is life a test or a continuous assessment? Does one face vivas on a daily basis or is group work more important? Should one examine knowledge and skills as encountered outside the classroom—more like those demanded in the office, the factory, and the store?

Should students be allowed to choose their assessment method? Or even indicate a preference? Discuss.

Executive teams

While onlookers seem more concerned with the personality and ability of the CEO, we know that it is the make-up and dynamics of the board of directors than can make all the difference to organizational performance.

Each with their special training, domain, and responsibility, these individuals, typically between six and twelve in number, hectically steer the organizational ship across stormy and unpredictable seas.

But ask any ex-board member, or indeed 'process' consultants called in to 'help with misunderstandings,' and they tell of politics and pathology, intrigue and infamy, skullduggery and spin. The first among equals may command most attention, but the board is crucial for decision-making, analysis, and strategy.

What are the typical problems of executive teams and how to deal with them? The first and most common is *bloated membership*. Everybody wants to sit on the board and be 'in the top team.' It is sexy, well paid, and a job with power.

There is an optimum number for efficient teamwork: somewhere between seven and twelve. Too big and teams split into factions; a few members become silent and others very vocal. It is, of course, also very important that those on the board bring not only their expertise and ability, but also their motivation to succeed through appropriate cooperation. It is all very well having the optimum number, but unless they pull together in the process the board will not succeed.

Any CEO needs to be clear about who is on the board *and why*. Is there an HR specialist on the board? Are there non-executive directors? Is some minority tokenism required?

These are non-trivial questions that need to be answered with analysis and logic. Such decisions have consequences.

The second issue can be the *naked ambition* of the many team members. Many yearn for the top job, head honcho. They see their career clocks ticking and feel the urge for the money, power, and prestige of the chief executive. Succession planning can bring out into the open and help control blind ambition. The team needs to specify a timetable, personal criteria for the top job, and the process by which the boss is appointed.

It is important the process is open, explicit, and apparently fair. Nepotism, pusillanimous chair-people, even laziness are reasons for massive boardroom squabbling. If it is the most important job then serious attention needs to be paid to appoint the right person.

The third issue is the *conspiracy of silence*. Big boys often cope with issues by never mentioning them. Teams often deal with emotional issues by ignoring them. Boards can refuse to discuss issues they find uncomfortable, such as success planning, personal pathology, relationships at work, or the future of the company. Anything to do with personal emotions is usually out of bounds. No evidence of emotional intelligence here.

It is surprising how powerful adults resort to such primitive influence and coping strategies to deal with issues.

The way to stop groups conspiring to be silent is to help them put the issues on the table. There needs to be a rule about what can and cannot be discussed, when, and why. It is often the personal pathology and interpersonal skills of the CEO that dictate what is taboo and what is not.

Consultants who deal with top-team pathology or boardroom malaise are often astounded by the history of 'non-discussables.' Interestingly, it is often tough professional women—so often missing from boards—that deal with the problem best. It is an issue of EQ not IQ ... and real balls.

A fourth issue is *resisting centrifugal forces*. Board members can, quite literally, head off in different directions. Their values and priorities can soon lead to the executive team losing its cohesiveness and focus.

This is most frequently the problem where individuals have difficulty delegating. Thus directors manage, managers supervise, supervisors deliver. Delegation should liberate board members to concentrate on what they do: strategy, the vision thing, PR on the part of everybody, and doing the rounds.

The CEO must become aware of the existence and power of these forces upon the members and, therefore, encourage uniformity of approach. Members need constant help with the focus and alignment.

A fifth problem is not unique to top teams but can be very destructive; it refers to the *ambiguity of roles*. Executive team members are answerable to many different constituencies. Executives need to specify very clearly *how* the group is to make decisions and what those decisions are about. What is, and is not, their remit. And once clarified, stick to it.

The sixth problem is the personal, but not *hidden agendas of individuals*. The boardroom is an ideal place, some believe, to have fun, to promote personal causes, to ride hobby horses. To have important and powerful people pay attention to their personal issues is too attractive an opportunity to miss for some directors, whose politico-religious or other crypto-philosophical agendas can hijack board meetings for hours.

The solution is quite simply to have a clear agenda and keep to it. Boards need to be told on a regular basis what they are there for. And what is not relevant.

It is too easy to see the problems of the board in terms of the lack of ability or simply pathology of the individual members. Some directors do make it to board level with remarkably mediocre ability. Others have exploited their particular personal pathology, such as narcissism or paranoia, to rise in the organization. But it is to be hoped they remain yet the minority—though, in some companies, this is far from clear.

It is the role of the chairperson to get the best out of the board through optimum membership, appropriate control and openness, getting members focused, clarifying their role and joint agenda. Sounds easier said than done with self-important grown-ups, but it is essential to ensure successful board functioning. The puzzle is why it is not done that often.

Fantastic futures

Business futurology: a weird and wacky world of fantastic nonsense or wise portender of tomorrow ... and the day after that? Futurologists can be categorized in many ways, but perhaps the most obvious dimension on which they fall is optimistic–pessimistic.

The doom merchants often get most attention. Their message is of destabilization and fragmentation. Of geopolitical disruption and global storms. Of institutional collapse and the clash of civilizations.

The pessimists see on the one hand the withering of the power, even the purpose of the state. They point out the unstoppable flow of people, goods, money, and information across borders. Bad for dictators but problematic, too, for democracies. There is at once political and business integration and disintegration.

All institutions are in disarray, from those we trust most to those we trust least. There is more multi-culturalism but nobody knows what it really means. Security is top of every agenda: government, business, private lives. Old countries, old industries are running out of time and losing their sense of direction. Everything we know and trust is under threat. It is the bleakness of Orwell's *Nineteen Eighty-Four* with ever present cameras and spy satellites monitoring one's every move.

The past looks so simple, so secure, so safe. There seems to be remorseless, even pointless change. And what most of us have learnt is that the only one who really likes change is a wet baby. The future looks so uncertain, so dark. And yet the futurologists never claim that it is unpredictable.

But the optimists believe the only scarce resource in the

future is creativity and ideas. Hence all that knowledge management tosh.

These optimists talk of organizations of the future with radically different jobs. More important than the CEO or CFO will be the CIO—the Chief Imagination Officer. There will be other new job titles, like director of mind and mood, intangible asset appraiser and assistant story teller. Their role is the very opposite of the old command-and-control stuff. Their job is to stimulate, direct, and control creative ideas.

Success in the future for countries will not depend on their manufacturing power or military might; it won't depend on their creativity and imagination.

Recall all the dotcom fantasies. The web will make everything possible, everything easy, and everything fun. All the drudgery of the past will disappear. Alas, all that really disappears is the dotcommers themselves.

Whether you are a naive optimists or gloomy pessimist it seems impossible not to recognize three major influences. Technology has changed, and is changing, the world. Faxes, libraries, and films are dead. What is next, and what influence will have it? Populations are changing: there are pensioner time-bombs in some countries and hoards of young unskilled workers in others. And globalization is a fact.

There is, and will be, much more distributed work. Many people—read skilled, educated, young—will have more choice over where, when, and what they do to be employed. Local regions, communities, and agencies, more than governments, will create (or shun) jobs in the future. Managers may have to be seen as work enablers and facilitators rather than controllers.

Some of the old questions have not been answered. Is there still pointless, illegal employment discrimination against certain groups? Is workplace stress simply hype and a result of litigious individuals in bed with the stress industry? Are modern workplaces physically safe? How and why can we integrate the long-term alienated jobless back into the workforce? Should we be eager to separate or blend the work–life divide? Can we learn much from forgiveness? Is the career dead? Will work in the future be more intrinsically satisfying, and for whom?

BULLYING AT WORK

Is bullying really on the increase at work? Or is it simply over-reporting by incompetent, lazy, vengeful staff, eager to punish their bosses and sue their organizations? Or does the stress and complexity of modern business life lead to stressed managers who then bully, harass, and victimize innocent and vulnerable workers?

Bullying is usually defined in terms of the duration, frequency, and intentionality by people in positions of power to unduly accuse, criticize, or humiliate others. For most adults, bullying is a psychological rather than a physical process, though of course it can be both. In essence, at work it is the abuse of power, though victims can also be bullied by peers and subordinates.

One central question for those interested in the whole issue is whether bullying can or should be explained by organizational, personality, or social factors. That is, does the organization condone or even promote bullying as a management technique? Or is there something about the make-up (personality, intelligence, social skills) of both bullies and their victims that leads them to seek each other out for their bizarre and beastly rituals? Or is it the social factors at work that lead to, or indeed prevent, bullying?

Certainly, bullying is more likely to occur in some environments rather than others: where there is role conflict or ambiguity; where there is acute or chronic work overload; where workers have little autonomy; where there is an atmosphere of fear of redundancy, or sacking, or whole organization collapse. In these circumstances bullying is more likely to happen. Whenever there is win/lose not win/win as a philosophy there is conflict and, often, in the shadows, lurks bullying.

Furthermore, some organizations have a history of autocratic leaders whose style becomes not only acceptable but required. None of that consultative, democratic nonsense with the authoritarian leader who admires strength.

Authoritarians demand rigid adherence to rules, an

uncritical acceptance of authority and a strong, open, aggressive condemnation of the weak, the outsider, or those who do not obey the rules. Many project their inner emotions and impulses onto others and have a sort of free-floating, generalized feeling of anger and hostility. Authoritarian leaders admire power and toughness. They have a preoccupation with dominance over others.

But what of the personality make-up of both bullies and their victims? Various groups do not want this discussed or researched because it might do two things they do not want. First, it might indicate that the bullied, as well as the bully are to blame for the situation. Second, it might imply that very little can be done to remedy bullying, because personality is difficult to change.

There has been a lot of research, both in schools and the workplace, on the vulnerable personality who is likely to be bullied, and the provocative personality who is likely to end up being the bully. And there are no surprises. Bullied people tend to be less stable, more anxious, and depressed. They also tend to have low emotional intelligence and few social skills, which means they find it harder to make and keep friends. They tend always to avoid conflict, to be submissive, and to be passive. And they have poor coping skills, such that they are both supersensitive to bullying and unable to cope adequately when bullied.

And, yes, bullies are in the playground, on the shop floor, and in the boardroom: aggressive, competitive, impulsive. They aren't too good at being assertive, either. Bullies are aggressive, the bullied are passive; neither seem very assertive.

But is all this research flawed? Does not the bullying experience change the individual? Is not the neurosis of the bullied a consequence rather than a cause of bullying? Does this personality research not amount to victim blaming and perpetrator condoning?

While it is true that the victims of bullying do appear to share various personality traits, there are differences between them. And we have little evidence from the bullied being tracked over time to sort out the cause-and-effect direction.

Everyone agrees with three issues. First, bullying is a serious problem that blights people's lives and affects workplace efficiency. Next, there are things we can do to prevent it—though some just mask it, others might increase it, and some genuinely help. Third, it is a multi-causal problem—that is, it has multiple causes. Bullying is likely to arise from various factors happening at the same time.

It is therefore just as unwise to ignore individual difference correlates of bullying as it is to insist that they are the predominant cause.

Generations at work

Some call them generations, others cohorts. And they have very different names: they may be called traditionalists or old fogies, baby boomers or the spoilt-60s generation. Then there is generation X, that often lamented lost generation, and the hopeful millennials.

Generations are distinguishable most by their attitudes and values, which have been shaped by their personal experiences. Growing up at a particular time and place often leaves a very strong mark on individuals. After all, societies try to socialize people into a set of beliefs and values about all the big issues: right/wrong, good/bad, just/unjust, fair/unfair.

Most people within a cohort fail to see the power of the forces on them that shape their views. They see only differences and variability between themselves, often unaware of the similarities. Paradoxically, they see other generations as 'all the same' and often treat them with suspicion, not noticing how varied they are. In psychobabble this is called 'out-group homogeneity' and 'in-group heterogeneity.'

Inevitably, generational differences play out in the workplace. Popularist social sciences have developed names for various seemingly identifiable groups. Thus we have traditionalists, baby boomers, generation X-ers, and millennials.

Traditionalists are products of the safe and secure 1950s. They were and are cautious, conformist, conservatives. They prefer structure and security. They understand loyalty and the career. They weren't (and aren't) very mobile and therefore had little experience of any type of diversity. They knew and accepted class divisions inside and outside work, and experienced relatively little technological change.

The baby boomers were shaped by the turbulent 1960s, when they challenged the assumptions and what they saw to be the complacency of their elders. This was the generation of civil rights, Woodstock, the moon landings, sit-ins, hijackings, and nuclear power.

The baby boomers were anti-conformist and anti-hierarchical. They did not like uniforms or uniformity. They were happy to experiment. And many enjoyed shocking others. They were rebels with a cause. And they were often disruptive at work. They distrusted authority and liked change for change's sake.

Generation X-ers were shaped by the turbulent times of the 1970s and 1980s. They experienced the worst depression since the 1930s. They saw the rise of the women's movement, the green movement, and the end of the manufacturing industry. They also witnessed the massive advances in computer technology and use. More importantly, they saw mass unemployment and compulsory redundancy.

Generation X-ers often got a bad press at work. They were neither conformist nor anti-conformist. If anything, they tended to be alienated. They felt little loyalty to those who expressed little loyalty to them. They were the 'me' not the 'we' generation who were told 'greed is good.' They saw the world at work as a jungle, and survival of the fittest as the name of the game.

Millennials joined the world of work around the year 2000. They had been shaped by the 1990s: the end of the USSR, the reunification of Germany, the end of apartheid, and most of all: globalization. Technology shrank the world and therefore profoundly affected it. Businesses chased the cheapest labor force, whether through increasing numbers of legal or illegal migrants, or simply by relocating factories and call centers in different parts of the world. Diversity at work wasn't an option—it was a reality and a necessity.

And machines replaced people. People became nomads:

they hot-bunked without offices, working out of their cars, hotel rooms, and sheds at the bottom of their gardens. Email replaced snail mail, cameras recorded one's comings and goings, and pensions were threatened.

Different generations have very different expectations of the world of work.

Going into sales

Unlike Americans, the British seem to have a rather low opinion of sales people and, on TV in particular, they are portrayed as somewhat shady characters. The President of the New York Stock Exchange realized this. Robert Whitney wrote: 'Salesmanship is an American specialty. It typifies the competitive spirit of our economy. Nowhere else in the world have so many executives come up through the selling ranks.'

This attitude may have cost the Brits dear. Think of all the things we invented that others then made into viable, commercial, saleable products. Why is inventiveness superior to selling? What's the purpose of brilliant design without brilliant marketing?

Few dispute the fact that successful sales people are both rare and often uniquely talented. They have insight, skill, and charm. They are perceptive, persuasive, and productive. They sell solutions, not just products. They understand how to form relationships fast, and how to close deals.

It certainly seems to be the case that a very large number of British CEOs have come up the accountancy route, while many American equivalents are ex-marketers.

This is not to confuse marketers and sales people. Indeed, the former often resent this shotgun marriage, where the marketers seem to have 'married beneath them.'

So whence the British snobbery about sales? There are perhaps two or three main reasons. First, sales does not seem to be a vocation. There are no degrees in sales, whereas there certainly are in marketing. Sales courses are short and sweet. You learn on the job. A bit like journalism. It's a honed skill, not an intellectual activity.

Going into sales

Unlike most jobs, there is a very weak relationship between intelligence and success at sales, at least at the coalface level. But, of course, senior sales people have to do the same business planning, strategy, and number tumbling as all senior managers. Some can't hack it—they prefer to be in the face-to-face selling business. That's fine—good for them and their company. And they may get immensely rich at it.

The few educational requirements mean that anyone can 'drift' into sales. No parent is overjoyed if their (albeit feckless) teenager admits he or she wants to become an insurance or estate agent. These are seen as dubious activities, for cads and bounders, not real gentlemen. It's not that they are all rogues and vagabonds, but rather they somehow don't deserve their rewards. It also challenges the most holy of holies: the class system.

A sales job is classless. Your origins, your education, your daddy do not count. You are on commission and it's entirely up to you. It's about aptitude and perseverance, not privilege. They are all there in sales: PhDs and failed college students; the offspring of both noblemen and garbage men; from families steeply upwardly or downwardly mobile. So American dream—so un-British.

The British seem to distrust sales people: they don't tell the truth. Worse, it's seen to be easy and somehow unearned money. Sales people do not really deserve the dosh they earn.

But think of what it requires to be really successful in sales. It takes energy and organization. It takes charm and determination. It takes perseverance and innovation. It takes resilience and fortitude. Are those not highly desirable characteristics in a CEO? Very much so.

Some people believe every successful executive should have the experience of various employment activities to be any good at their job. Three seem particularly important: acting, counseling, and selling. Some organizations have dispensed with those enormously expensive mini MBAs.

Instead, they send their aspirant wunderkinds on three week-long courses. One is on acting—understanding and portraying the human condition. This is really good for public speaking and media interviews. Next, there's a counseling course, doing a stint on helplines, which refines EQ, teaches compassion and how to listen and, sometimes, humility. And the third is sales—cold calling telesales, even selling insurance or double glazing.

And it is the last of these that may be really diagnostic. Is it too dramatic or completely unfair to argue that if you can't sell you can't manage? Probably. But if you can't sell ideas, you can't sell enthusiasm, you can't sell change, you really won't do well at running the show.

Does this mean that all CEOs are vacuous, garrulous, shallow extroverts? Of course not. These really are inappropriate stereotypes attached to people in sales. Very British. Very wrong. So welcome some sales experience on the CV. It may be a really good indicator of a dynamic, persuasive, and go-for-it executive.

Guru-busting

Gurus of self-appointed management, work–life balance, and sales techniques are two a penny. Futurologists are a new growing breed (or should that be virus). Emotion science may be the next fad.

It is said that journalists use the word guru only because they cannot spell charlatan. Gurus multiply according to market forces. Cost-to-entry is low. The media are hungry for new ideas. Managers are desperate. Personal marketing is cheap. So gurus flourish.

So how to differentiate between the perspicacious and profound pundit and the blarney and baloney of the bull-shitter?

The following ten points may be useful in trying to separate the wheat from the chaff.

1. Beware and check gurus' academic training. Be particularly and paradoxically suspicious of those who protest too much about their academic qualifications. A sure sign that a business book is both evidence-free and jargon-infected is that the author has PhD after his name on the cover. Remember, doctorates can be earned from 'life experience' and bought from Bogus State University, Nowhereville.

2. Beware also the other signs of impression management: the ostentatious *FT* or *Wall Street Journal* tucked under the arm, and conspicuous use of state-of-the-art electronic gizmos that have little to do with data gathering or analysis. They are the tricks and toys of mind readers, fortune tellers, and their fellow travelers. They are there to distract, to embellish, not to inform or help.

3. Beware the metaphor, the analogy, and the parable. They often serve to confuse and obfuscate. Case studies may be a good way of teaching medical and business students but beware the overuse of some simple-minded analogy. Balanced scorecards, flying fish, cheese-eating mice, and empty raincoats take us only so far ... and no further.

4. Listen to explanations (not descriptions) of process. Consultants must move past descriptions and tautology, and provide clear explanations for the causes of issues at work. Be particularly sensitive to contradictions, fuzzy logic, missing steps. Treatment follows diagnosis. Diagnosis must come after thorough, consistent, disinterested examination of the problem.

5. Change strategies, interventions, and the like must follow exactly from the diagnosis. They must be consistent. The guru must explain how that strategy has that particular effect. Beware fuzzy-thinking, 'just trust me' magic, where semi-mystical intervention strategies supposedly have immediate, powerful, long-lasting, and even contradictory effects.

6. Check whether gurus can write. Can they use clear, jargon-free, correct language to explain how they see the problem and the solution? Criticize sloppy writing, the use of pseudo-scientific jargon, and the preference for presentation over documentation.

7. Determine whether gurus have any depth of knowledge or understanding about all the social issues that have an impact on business. This must include a rudimentary understanding of political and economic issues. They must move on from glib name-dropping of book titles and slang from other gurus' books.

8. Gurus love to tell stories: stories with happy endings; stories of overjoyed clients; stories of management and workers walking arm in arm to an ever productive

sunset. A sort of modern-day equivalent of those grey Stalinist Stakhanovite workers who were the crudest of propaganda. Again, the more fabulous the stories, the more the fable, and the greater the likelihood you are being foxed.

9. Gurus don't like particulars in two senses. They don't like the idea of having to adapt, adjust, even change an idea, a concept, an intervention because of particular unique circumstances. They also don't like details. They tend to be broad-brush, pan-cultural, all-sectors types, who feel that bespoke stuff is difficult, time wasting and unprofitable.

10. If you suspect that any advice, fad, or 'theory' is bunkum, it nearly always is. Skepticism, not cynicism, is a very healthy yardstick by which to measure the integrity, and veracity, of any guru. Real ones are rare. A good rule of thumb is about 12 to 1. That is, for every 12 proclaimed gurus, 1 is worth listening to. And when it comes to self-proclaimed gurus, the ratio may drop from 12 to 1 to nearly 100 to 1. So, as ever, caveat emptor.

Happiness myths

There are three pervasive and dangerous myths about happiness at work. They distort management thinking and practice. They are not based on research, and they have a serious negative effect on the organization.

- Myth 1: Happy workers are productive workers.
- Myth 2: Happiness can be found, taught, or acquired.
- Myth 3: It is the duty and responsibility of the organization to guarantee the happiness of its staff.

If you believe Myth 1 you spend a great deal of effort trying to increase staff morale, satisfaction, or whatever you want to call it, in the naive hope that this will logically lead to greater productivity and profit. So you spend money on designer offices or superior canteen facilities. You institute work–life balance, family-friendly arrangements, and have a crèche.

There have been countless studies over the years looking at the correlations between satisfaction and productivity. The better ones have tried to separate cause and correlation. And the results: weak, ambiguous, and contradictory. Some do show that if you increase satisfaction productivity does increase. But there are three problems. First, it is not necessarily proportional. That is, if you increase satisfaction by, say, 3 points (on an imaginary 20-point scale) that does not necessarily mean that productivity goes up the same amount. Next, an increase in work-based satisfaction can be very temporary. See the effect of giving people a pay rise: yes, it has an effect, but a very short-lived one. Third, there may well be a limit to both satisfaction and productivity, particularly if the latter is powerfully related to technology, competition, processes, or supplier.

In fact, there is just as much evidence to suggest that productivity causes satisfaction. The productive worker is a rewarded worker, with better pay and promotion prospects. Not always, granted, but often enough. Teach people how to be more productive. Make sure they have the right tools, processes, and teamwork for the job. And watch them become happier.

Many of even the best-conducted studies show no relationship between satisfaction and productivity. Why? The obvious answer is that both are multi-determined. An individual's productivity is related to other personal characteristics (ambition, health, intelligence) and also business processes. Small changes in process can have much bigger effects on productivity than tinkering with happiness/satisfaction ideas.

Myth 2 is that happiness can be acquired. Just as intelligence cannot be acquired, so happiness seems remarkably stable over time and resistant to change. There are, in short, happy and unhappy people. Happy people remain so even after trauma; and unhappy people even with countless blessings. One study showed that quadriplegics (such as the late Christopher Reeve) 'reverted' to their natural level of happiness two years after their accident. A similar study of lottery winners found the same.

Beware the happiness industry. Beware those with the inalienable right to pursue happiness. Happiness is the holy grail. Happiness is a trait, a disposition. There are DNA markers of it. Sure, you can make people really unhappy. And you can give people temporary happiness. But study people in prisoner of war camps or even *Big Brother* and you will that see some are constantly cheery, optimistic, positive … and others are not. And overall it is better to be surrounded by the positive than the negative. Happy people are as life-enhancing as unhappy people are hard going. Both can affect the tone of teams.

If you want and like happy people, select and recruit them. Make optimism a core competency. Ask about it in references. Beware Job's comforter: they can suck you dry of enthusiasm.

Myth 3 is also widely held. Just as it is not the responsibility of an organization to make people moral, good, or healthy, so it is not its responsibility to try to change happiness levels. If an organization tried to convert people to a set of explicitly religious beliefs or a particularly sexually oriented lifestyle, there would be outrage. People have a private out-of-work life that is their business.

It is the job of employers to ensure people are safe, healthy, and productive at work. It is the task of managers to ensure work is done efficiently and effectively; that, where appropriate, profits (or surpluses) are made; that the organization survives the slings and arrows of outrageous fortune and thrives. If an organization fails at these tasks people leave. They need help, respect, goals, support, and feedback.

But management should not try to guarantee happiness at work. Call it subjective well-being or hedonic level—it is all the same thing. Work tasks and demands can cause stress and, over time, long-term unhappiness, even in the dispositionally happy. But people soon leave that situation.

The task of the manager is to focus on process and product: to maximize the former to produce the latter. Managing happiness in individuals is not only irrelevant but impossible.

Hidden persuaders

Nearly 50 years ago an American writer called Vance Packard argued that, by using subliminal cues, advertisers and marketers persuaded people to buy against their will. The theory is that people can be emotionally and behaviorally affected by visual or vocal stimuli whose presence they do not report.

Whether it is preconscious processing or unconscious perception, few psychologists dispute or would even be surprised by the idea that people can be affected by stimuli they claim not to have seen. What people say they saw and did see are not the same.

By flashing up images and words very quickly, scientists have been able to demonstrate reliably the process called subliminal perception. But—and it is a very big but—there is very little evidence that subliminal perception then influences a person's attitudes, beliefs, choices, and motives. There is, in short, no reliable scientific evidence that subliminal perception has any behavioral impact or effect on intentions.

But lack of evidence has never got in the way of a good theory. So down the years journalists and popular authors have argued that some, even most, advertisements contain hidden sexual images or particular brand names or messages that affect our susceptibility to those advertisements. So the attention-grabbing, paranoid, but evidence-free myth goes: clever (wicked) advertisers can make you do things against your better judgment, conscious decision-making or will, by subliminal messages in (mainly television, but also radio) ads. Careful research has suggested that this idea is absurd or laughable and ludicrous, paranoid and preposterous.

Conspiracy theories always make good copy. We have moved on from *Nineteen Eighty-Four*-type conspiracy to commercial conspiracy. Big companies, staffed by audacious, foreign capitalists are heartlessly abusing us, particularly the naive and gullible. They supposedly have the power to render us into performing mannequins and puppets.

We know that advertisements use visuals or vocal words or themes to encourage us to make connections between brands, products, and particular behaviors and emotions. We also know that advertisements may well influence attitudes and values without people's awareness. But this is not subliminal advertising.

From the late 1950s to the mid-1970s, books with titles like *Subliminal Seduction* and *Media Sexploitation* kept the notion alive for a public apparently happy to see wicked manipulative scientists working with greedy, cynical advertisers. Shopaholism, suicides, and sexual disorders were all seen to be partly consequences of this conspiracy.

But clever sales people did see the positive side of the public's gullibility. They knew from their research that subliminal advertising did not work … and was, anyway, both illegal and illogical. But why not turn the whole thing around and openly sell the technique? Hey presto! We have subliminal auditory self-help tapes.

Soon tapes were on sale that showed dramatic changes in mental and psychological health. You simply set the tape recorder to go off while you were asleep and you could experience weight loss, improved sexual function, ease in stopping smoking or nail biting, or conquering fear of flying. Tapes came in various forms. Some were designed to be played while awake. But they all had those subliminally embedded messages that you could not pick up but that could change your life.

So the modality changed from visual to auditory and the image of the science from wicked to helpful. Scientists got to work on this one, testing the claim that an undetectable speech signal changes behavior. It is a stronger claim that if critical messages are masked (drowned or washed out) by other sounds, the weak becomes detected, then disentangled, then comprehensible.

Tapes provide a pipeline to the id—that Freudian concept of the primitive persona, which is a cauldron of seething excitement. They can, it is claimed, get to the deepest parts of our being.

But scientists have tested these assumptions carefully. The jury is back. There is no evidence for these theoretically jumbled claims. This is therefore not only quackery but fraud: the advertisements have the obvious intention to deceive people who want a fast, cheap 'cure' involving little will power or pain.

And herein lies the paradox. Scientific evidence is often full of caveats and not written in everyday, easily accessible language. Scientists write for each other. Scientists might be unanimous in their evidence-based opinion that subliminal tapes make fraudulent claims, but they don't seem too hot at getting their message across.

On the other hand, the commercially savvy tape producers have commissioned advertising agencies to design new campaigns. Using scientific jargon and imagery, and the power of repetition, the aggressive campaigns have succeeded in keeping the myths alive. Ironic that traditional advertising succeeds in selling subliminal tapes that don't persuade.

It's so hard to beat pseudoscience and superstition with skepticism and science.

Hitting targets

The British police, it seems, are to be given financial bonuses for hitting pre-set targets with respect to crime figures and recruitment from minority ethnic groups. And why not? Struggle to get crime down and be rewarded for it. Set clear goals, give feedback and a reward commensurate with effort and outcome. The essence of good management ... or is it?

Performance management systems have replaced the old time-in-service reward systems. Instead of being promoted on years of service and loyalty, what is now important is management by objectives, 'achieving targets' as it is known.

There are, however, problems with these systems and the whole thing can seriously backfire if you are not careful. Try to find any organization where the majority of the staff are happy with their performance management system. Often introduced with the hype and spin of modernity and state-of-the-art management practice, they are often quietly withdrawn as they cause nothing but problems.

There are four reasons why they run into problems. The first is *measurement of targets*. How accurate, sensitive, and reliable are these measures? Are they done by a manager, or a customer, or the employees themselves? Can they be tweaked, are they in the gift of managers, or are they 'hard facts'?

The second problem lies in the equity of the system: are all people measured and rewarded equally? If the rewards are based on hitting targets you have to measure the *individual's contribution*. This can have a very negative effect on teamwork. In fact, it may encourage competition when what is really needed is cooperation.

The third problem lies in the *control* that individuals have in reaching those targets. If hitting a target or achieving a goal is primarily the result of random events like the weather, or the economy, or powerful figures like politicians, it can become extremely frustrating for the individual. It means that whatever ability they have or effort they put in, they may well easily miss their targets. This can replace a sense of instrumentalistic 'can do' with a spirit of hopeless fatalism.

But the fourth, and by far the most important, question is what desirable and undesirable *behaviors result* directly from the targets themselves. Consider two examples: traffic wardens and bus drivers.

How should you reward traffic wardens? Some towns make them wear pedometers and check that they have 'walked their beat' a certain number of times a day. Make that the only measure and they wander around aimlessly even in the rain. Make the criterion the number of tickets given out and wardens issue them constantly, viciously, and unfairly, with little regard to the traffic flow consequences or the special circumstances of the individual who may dispute the parking offence. Make the criterion revenue generated per ticket and they go all out for high-value tickets—that is, more rather than less serious offences. Make the success criterion a mix of variables and behavior changes accordingly. If you were to penalize them for issuing tickets that were later successfully challenged, they would take more care. It is only lawyers who get rich from court cases.

Bus drivers drive differently depending on their targets. Is it revenue per full journey, or customer satisfaction as determined by random interviews, or is it being on schedule? Make time the only criterion and drivers behave like mad people on the edge of the law, with scant regard for the welfare of their passengers.

Targets do change behavior. Rewards and punishments do work. The taxman knows that well. The present British

Government certainly takes a *homo economicus* view of its citizens, believing they respond perfectly to financial rewards and punishments.

A few years ago, British people complained that the police seemed reticent to record certain crimes. Why? Possibly because they knew that 'clear up' rates were so low for some types of crimes which were performance targets. Solution: reduce recorded crime and performance apparently improves. Equally, many motorists believe they are easy targets. Some worry that the previously police-supporting middle class is becoming rapidly alienated as a result of the way motoring offence targets are set and measured.

The moral: measurement and reward change behaviors in ways not always anticipated. Think through the consequences of setting any targets for the boys in blue.

How to become a guru

Ever fancied giving up the day job for money, fame, or excitement? Ever wanted to fly first class? To have thousands pitch up to listen to your every word? To charge a five-figure sum for less than a day's work? Ever wanted to appear on television, be interviewed by print journalists, and invited to meet important people who believe you could help them?

You have? The answer is simple—become a business guru. The field is competitive, but there is still room if you have what it takes.

So where to start? You need an instruction manual and a tool kit, and a survival guide that sets out the stages fairly logically. You may not have to change you name, but certainly your dress, style of speech, manner, and so on. You need to be a bit quirky, a bit funky, but not 'out of the box.' You probably need a serious make-over by another guru—a style guru. This guru-to-guru consultation is itself useful as it models guru behavior. However, this presentational stuff really should come later. It follows, not precedes, the fundamental business of having a theory, a model—a silver bullet.

The process starts with an idea to fill a need. What are the major problems of business today? Worker morale? Absenteeism? Accidents? Quality control? Customer response time? These problems are probably complex, intractable, and interrelated. But never let that stop you. Focus on one problem that is widespread, costly, and contemporary in its focus. Now offer a simple, counter-intuitive solution.

The solution needs a sexy name. Something that fits the zeitgeist. Good prefixes might be 'bio' or 'hyper' or 'quantum.' And good suffixes might include 'ology' or 'phy.'

So just as we had process re-engineering we now need bio-behavioral transformation or linear sequential processing. Three short words work well, as does alliteration. So how about entropic entrepreneurial eschatology, financial fusion, or transcendental thru-pulling.

Once you have the brand name you need to explain the process. You need a technique or invention or method, and it needs to be backed up with some sort of theoretical explanation.

But don't worry about all that business data, proof, science, and so forth. Fashion's past all that now: it's post-modernity time. So, say with the through-a-glass-darkly merchants: 'the old science of observation and experiment failed us. You are working within the new paradigm. That is real innovation.'

This is important because you must claim that the old science can't really test your theory or method … otherwise you are really in trouble. Scorn the past. Scorn the management scientists with their reductionist, rat-based, obsolete paradigm. You are part of the new wave, the revolution, and your method and theory are spearheading the new world.

Bring along happy customers. Tell grand tales of saving whole companies from death and destitution. Rejoice in parable telling … they are called 'case studies' and they really are all the proof you'll ever need.

But you have to learn to be a showman. Take lessons in acting and rhetoric. Charisma can (sort of) be learnt. You need presence. You need to be able to read cues. You need, most of all, the ability to spin. Listen to top politicians answering questions. Tune into those strange American TV evangelists. Watch pop stars. They are all fine models for your art. And never shirk debate. It's good PR. Attack, don't defend. And go for a bit of new-wave mysticism, anti-materialism, and remember the limitations of reason.

Be ready with a bit of conspiracy theory, too. They attack you not because of your ideas, but your race, parents, language, or sexuality. Remember there are powerful, evil, international consortia that have a vested interest in preventing you telling your story that will help millions. Remember you are the altruist; they are the bad guys out to get you.

And remember to be both expensive and difficult as a consultant. Demand special things; your Thai masseur, your Romanian mineral water. And don't think twice about a five-figure fee for a day's work. After all, you are saving the company (and possibly the world).

Remember along the way a number of well-established lessons: the power of placebo; people believe that expensive things are good; some processes are mysterious and mystical; charisma convinces.

Oh yes—you probably have to produce books, videos, and the like, but that is not too difficult. There is an army of tabloid ghost writers there to help you.

The shelf-life of a guru—the word used by journalists because they can't spell charlatan—is often short. More than 15 minutes of fame. But huge fun and hugely profitable. You know you are up to it, worth it and will, after all, do such a lot of good. And, who knows, you may even save the world!

Humor at work

The death of a well-known and beloved comic actor affects many people. To laugh with (not at) somebody who somehow encapsulates and makes fun of the human condition with all its foibles is indeed good for the soul.

Recently the relationship between humor and health has been established both at the individual and the organizational level. Humor and laughter are, quite simply, good for you. Laughter lowers blood pressure and oxygenates the blood, thereby increasing energy levels and the feeling of well-being. It reduces hormones released in response to stress and helps prevent lethargy. Furthermore, over time, it has been shown to boost the immune system. So it is true: laughter really is the best medicine.

The idea that humor and laughter may be good for people has not escaped managers and gurus. If it has been shown that humor provides short- and long-term positive emotional, social, and physiological effects, it is no surprise that business people are interested. If humor can reduce absenteeism and increase productivity we certainly need it. So do we have to hire humor consultants, or arrange humor workshops, and/or use humor as an essential competency in hiring and promotion decisions?

The business boffins say humor is an important stress-buster. To see the funny side of all those daft corporate activities does help. It keeps things in perspective and may even boost morale among the 'little people' who are often the victims of head-office madness.

Humor may have other functions. It can help engender a sense of playfulness, which in turn can help creativity. It can boost morale and help bind teams together. It certainly can help in social occasions like dreary meetings. It can defuse conflict, open up dialogues, and allow difficult and subtle things to be said, while allowing everyone to save face. It can help people connect quickly and build rapport. And it is particularly important in customer service situations.

Those blessed with a sense of humor seem to be able to do things with a lighter touch, to develop trust and to communicate more effectively than their humor-challenged colleagues. Or can they? The business hype about the use of humor at work may have forgotten something rather important: the politically correct police.

The problem is that humor may be rather idiosyncratic. Those who praise the use of humor seminars and workshops skip over this all-important point. What one person finds very funny either passes over or pisses off his or her colleagues.

Those psychologists interested in taxonomizing humor have found very different groups. Whether it is visual or verbal humor, there appear to be quite different categories of jokes and stories that are thought of as funny. Four groups seem very clear.

1. Nonsense humor: whether jokes, shaggy dog stories or cartoons, this relies on tricks like puns or incongruous, inconsistent situations.
2. Satire: this refers to jokes or stories that are funny because they are at the expense of and attempt to ridicule particular people, groups, organizations, or institutions.
3. Aggressive humor: this works for certain people and can show (particularly in cartoons) pictures of violence, torture, and even sadism, as well as verbal insults.
4. Sexual humor: this, of course, refers to subtle or explicit sexual jokes, from crude to vulgar depending on your taste.

It is, of course, possible to find other categories and split the groups above. Those social scientists that research humor have also been interested in the correlates of humor. Are there culture, gender, intelligence, and personality correlates of humor? Why does some humor not travel while other types seem universal? Do more intelligent people like puns and wordplay more than less intelligent people? Do people grow out of some types of humor?

But the use of any sort of humor has come under the spotlight because of the growing 'right of offence.' Tell a joke (from any of the above categories) and you can be sure someone somewhere will be offended. They may not like you, or perhaps they have had a sense of humor bypass, but it does not matter. They complain and instigate an investigation. And there is nothing as problematic as explaining a joke and why it is funny.

So humor has become more and more constrained and *verboten* in the workplace. Unless it is completely anodyne and therefore, by definition, not very funny, it may be very unwise to try humor to diffuse a situation or communicate something rather subtle. So whether it is funny ha-ha, funny peculiar, or funny pathetic, it is now unwise to say it.

Be very careful, then, with jokes, puns, and off-the-cuff remarks that are meant to be funny. It is too easy to offend and get into trouble these days. So, if in doubt, desist! Best keep to good jokes for those you know and trust, and who share your view of the world. And probably better to show and appreciate humor out of the workplace rather than in it.

Idealists and ideologies

Try the forced-choice test. Circle either a or b. Don't ponder, nit-pick, or dither.

1. (a) An individual's personality and make-up is primarily a product of their upbringing and social environment.

   (b) Human nature is pretty well innate and immutable.

2. (a) There are no innate ability differences among race, gender or age groups that might lead to differences in social status.

   (b) Fundamental differences in innate endowments between groups lead inexorably to differences in status.

3. (a) People are, by and large, rational.

   (b) Individuals are frequently irrational and a-rational, and behave in self-defeating ways.

4. (a) Human beings are, in a sense, perfectable and progress pretty well unlimited.

   (b) Social progress may be an illusion.

5. (a) Equalizing opportunities leads to benefits for all.

   (b) Social engineering is detrimental to historical, group, and individuals' identities and progress.

6. (a) Many of our existing social institutions must be changed or eliminated to ensure social progress.

   (b) We must preserve our great social institutions, which have stood the test of time.

There are two types of people in the world: those who believe there are two types and those who don't. One distinction is as old as the hills in the optimist–pessimist distinction. The half-full and half-empty brigade.

The heady days of the 1960s were when the social scientists were most optimistic and most change-oriented. Everything was possible because everything was environmentally determined. A person's ability, personality, health, and happiness were all (fairly simple) products of the social, economic, and political environment. Which can, with effort and political will, be changed.

Money should be poured into educational programs, not only to maximize a person's talents, but also to avoid (wicked and pernicious) inequality. Inequality of all sorts was perceived to be primarily a function of social and economic conditions.

Create the ideal environment—equal, moral, rational—and you get happy, healthy, contented people. Level playing field. Abolition of privilege. End to all those wicked 'isms' like racism, sexism, ageism. Of course, this endeavor may involve a radical restructuring of society.

The 1960s social scientists were optimistic revolutionaries. At the forefront of the fight. Believers in radical revisionism. And they had a vision of the New Jerusalem with everybody self-actualizing in nirvana. But reality clicked in. Money was wasted. People remained more or less as happy and unhappy, contented or discontented, productive or unproductive as ever. Differences in wealth and achievement did not diminish.

The social scientists were taken on by the biological scientists, whose genetic studies showed that things were as much nature as nurture. Furthermore, nature was nasty, selfish, and brute. People are not, never were, and never could be easily made into empathic, cooperative, giving individuals. They appear to be cruel, irrational, and bent entirely on protecting their own and feathering their own nest.

Socio-biologists and behavior geneticists have now provided incontrovertible evidence of the genetic origin of so many human conditions, from health to sex preferences, academic achievement to social beliefs and values. There are profound, stable, individual, as well as gender and race differences. And they affect all aspects of life.

This does not mean, and never has, that the environment/nurture position is now redundant. But it has taken the shine off those whose ideology is idealistic.

Impulsivity

Searching for the energetic, spontaneous, restless, impatient, quick decision-maker? Do you want a lively live-wire who gets on with it? But what about the impulsive, thrill-seeking, complexity-avoiding, easily distracted, unreflective manager, who can't and won't plan for the future? Surely they are worth avoiding? Trouble is, these traits go together. They form a cluster called 'impulsivity.'

Consider the ten simple statements below.

1. I often do things without thinking.
2. I am not very serious minded.
3. I usually make up my mind very quickly.
4. I generally seek new and exciting experiences and sensations.
5. I am pretty happy-go-lucky.
6. I can put my thoughts into words pretty quickly.
7. I admit I often lose interest in things I have started.
8. I get really impatient waiting.
9. I don't like and am not good at business planning.
10. I am not the person to 'sleep on it' before making a decision.

If you agreed with seven or more of these you would probably be called impulsive. This means your work is often fast but inaccurate. This may or may not matter ... depending on the task.

Impulsive people are often stable, and sociable, but not very conscientious. They prefer 'explosive' to 'endurance' sports. And they tend to have more traffic accidents and violations.

More interestingly, impulsives are highly sensitive to reward cues but curiously insensitive to punishment cues. This, in effect, means that they are better managed by promises of quick, sexy, exciting rewards than by the threat of dire punishment. Impulsivity can be exaggerated by caffeine and tends to be more noticeable in the evening than the morning.

The impulsive manager may have superficial appeal. They don't mess about, do take risks, and do embrace change. They go for quick rewards and seem to have limitless energy. They may thrive in certain worlds, like PR and advertising, where the pace and task demands fit their preferences.

There are benefits of what is called functional impulsivity. The functional (that is, good) impulsive can quickly take advantage of unexpected opportunities. They can rapidly put their thoughts into words. They can think on their feet. They are mentally agile. The bright functional impulsive is an asset; the dim one much less so.

But, equally, they can be lethal. They need someone to temper their enthusiasm, to consider consequences, to plan ahead and to keep persisting in the face of failure or setback. Impulsives need control mechanisms to moderate their fast tempo and love of reward. These mechanisms may lie in other aspects of their personality. Thus the brighter the impulsive the better—the more they see consequences and can size up a situation wisely. And the more anxiety prone (up to a point, of course) the better, because this tempers the risky recklessness that is so often associated with impulsives.

The dysfunctional impulsive can be an accident waiting to happen. These people say whatever comes into their heads without thinking first. They make appointments without checking they can honor them. They buy things before considering whether they can afford them. They jump in, just do it, before considering difficulties, implications, pros, and cons. They don't like careful reasoning.

So it's a trade-off. A bright, impulsive person in fast-moving products can be an advantage. But impulsivity, like all human characteristics, is normally distributed in a bell curve. Most of us have moderate impulsivity. So it's not a case of all or nothing. To be on the high side of the impulsivity spectrum brings its advantages and disadvantages. The adventurous, active, enthusiastic impulsive can bring dynamism to any group. But the disorderly, anti-analytic, planless impulsive can lead any well-thought-through plan to doom and destruction.

Just do it!

Procrastination may be the thief of time, but ill-considered decisions at work have costly consequences. Clearly there is an optimum time period for analysis, reflection, and consultation, and any resulting action. Too slow and cautious may reflect risk aversion and lead to missed opportunities. Too fast and furious may be because of an unwillingness or inability to do an appropriate business analysis. So, like everything else, one seeks the optimal solutions: the via media, the middle (not the third) way.

The question, of course, is why both individuals and organizations lean towards the sub-optimal. We all know the plodding, procrastinating, and perfectionist organization that takes ages to do anything. Individuals are both selected for and socialized into a culture of cautious consideration: 'Take your time and get it right,' 'Rome wasn't built in a day,' 'Everything comes to he who waits,' and other similar adages trip easily from the lips of people in these organizations.

'A good idea but a touch premature,' 'Interesting but untested,' 'Possible only in the fullness of time,' and 'With due diligence and full consultation' are the sort of brilliant put-down and piss-off phrases of the slow-and-steady brigade. They are to be found in all sectors, but they seem thicker on the ground in administration, health and safety, and research.

But in the fast-moving world of consumer goods and consultancy, fashion and advertising, speed is of the essence. There is less time for wise evaluation and full consideration. You have to get on with it, make a decision—even if all the information is not in—and take the risk. 'Just do it' is indeed a competency in some organizations.

A large part of the socialization of children is about reducing and controlling what psychologists call impulsivity. A related psychological concept is a postponement of gratification, and it is taken as an index of maturity. Children have to learn to wait, and to realize that it is better not to do everything now. Parents try to change pocket-money systems from a weekly basis to a monthly basis around puberty so that their offspring can learn to budget, to save, and to reap the rewards of investment.

The impulsive adult is often thought of as neither sophisticated nor polite. They eat in the street, seemingly unable to wait a few minutes before they get to an appropriate place. Their lack of impulse control is found particularly among delinquents of all ages, who want their drink, sex, tobacco, and other uppers and downers now.

It is not an issue of stoical self-denial. The non-impulsive may consume more than the more impulsive because, through wise saving and investment, they actually have more.

For years psychological researchers saw impulsivity as essentially a bad thing. Impulsive adults were rude, accident prone, and selfish. They tended to have brushes with the law and unhappy relationships, and rarely fulfilled their potential. Impulsivity was the enemy of self-control. Researchers in this topic have constructed various questionnaires designed to measure the extent of a person's impulsivity.

But relatively recently some academics have been bold enough to challenge the received wisdom about impulsive types, daring to suggest that there is functional and dysfunctional impulsivity. The latter is well known. Below are the sorts of behaviors that indicate its presence.

◆ Saying whatever comes into their head without thinking first.
◆ Acting before thinking of the consequences.

◈ Never planning, budgeting, or weighing up pros and cons appropriately.

However, the other side of the coin is interesting. Functional (healthy) impulsivity is characterized by the following.

◈ Taking advantage of unexpected opportunities by quick actions.
◈ Putting thoughts into words accurately.
◈ The ability to make, and feel comfortable with making, quick decisions.

So functional impulsivity is about being cognitively quick: the tendency to engage in rapid, error-prone information processing when this strategy is optimal. And there's the rub. The healthy impulsive knows when to exploit their speediness, the unhealthy impulsive does not. The former is flexible and sensitive, while the latter is not.

There is a time and a place for quick, but accurate, responses. And there is a time for careful consideration. The dysfunctional impulsive is a victim, not a fan of 'just do it' thinking. They can, in effect, do no other. They don't like thinking about it first, doing a SWOT analysis, or carefully considering all angles. Their childlikeness can become childishness.

The functional impulsive could be seen as the optimal performer in many business situations. No doubt they need to be bright and self-confident, too.

The dysfunctional impulsive makes social, logical, and business errors. Obsessives can't make their minds up in time and lose out on many opportunities. Step forward the functional impulsives: quick on their feet and quick in their head. Just do it!

BURNOUT, OUT BUT OPULENT

It's over a quarter of a century since the burnout concept at work was formulated. Initially it was thought that certain professionals were particularly prone to it: health care professionals, teachers, and the police. Those in remorseless, demanding, people-oriented jobs.

The early work focused on doctors, who were thought of as particularly prone because of the pressure of too many patients, having to make critical decisions based on ambiguous information, and having to face the consequences of those decisions. Furthermore, interaction with patients and their families and friends is often fraught because they are charged with anxiety, embarrassment, and tension. So this leads from acute to chronic stress, and thence to burnout.

Burnout is associated with physical exhaustion and illness, with increasing use of legal and illegal drugs, with marital and family conflict, as well as the usual suspects associated with neuroses: anxiety, depression, hypochondria, and low self-esteem. And this leads to feeling one has nothing left to give, that one has essentially achieved nothing, and that somehow it is one's clients (patients, students, customers) that are the cause of the problems.

There are physical, behavioral, and work performance indicators of burnout. Burnt-out people are prone to headaches, sleep disturbance, colds and flu, and skin and stomach problems. They may either lose weight or gain weight, depending on their personality. They certainly appear moody, grumpy, and suspicious. They make bad decisions and are easily frustrated. Many pop 'uppers and downers' to help with the tiredness. And they become dulled, dampened, and diminished in the workplace. They seem to work hard but not smart; to waste energy and bite everyone's heads off.

Those interested in burnout usually suggest that there are three distinguishable but related factors that make up the syndrome. The first is *exhaustion*. The burnt out report being physically and emotionally drained, about feeling 'all used up' with little more to give. They feel under constant strain, always tired. We all know the feeling, but for the burnt out it is both acute and chronic.

The second symptom *is cynicism*. The burnt out doubt if they really make any contribution and are hence less interested, enthusiastic, or committed to their job. They are more than alienated with a sense of anomie. They cannot be bothered. At work they are automata. They are cynical about management and peers, customers and subordinates—fast about anybody and everybody they come into contact with.

The third symptom is a total *lack of personal efficacy*. The effective employee can feel confident, competent, and considerate at work. They feel they accomplish worthwhile things, making a real contribution to their company, clients, friends, and family. They can report exhilaration at work and are really happy to be there. The burnt out never experience any of this. Indeed, their reaction is the precise opposite.

So what are the antecedents of burnout? The usual suspects are implicated: long work hours with a heavy 'psychological workload.' Work culture and a lack of decision authority were also implicated.

It seems that there are various reactions to burnout. Some people may actually feign burnout for ulterior motives, while others try to hide it. Equally, some organizations deny that it exists among their employees, while others appear to be happy to try to help the burnt out.

Easy enough to describe and diagnose, but what to do about it? Some jobs are not easy to change to reduce burnout, but things can be done to help those individuals more or less prone to succumbing.

Some organizations, aware of the pressure put on individuals, try hard to screen out the more vulnerable. Hardiness, not hard-heartedness, is a major prophylactic to burnout. People need to be resilient, to be able to keep their self-esteem in place when faced with personal criticism. Everyone has their tipping point, but some are more easily tipped than others.

So, select resilient people, put in place support mechanisms that are effective and acceptable to use, help staff to work smarter rather than harder, understand the benefits of play and relaxation … and neither sweep it under the carpet nor expect it to be commonplace in the organization.

Management desiderata

Once it was called 'work satisfaction,' then 'commitment,' and now 'engagement.' Its opposite is 'alienation,' estranged from all that happens in the workplace.

All managers want their staff to be fully committed to the aims of the organization, happy in their work, and totally engaged in what they are doing. So how to achieve engagement? Indeed, is it even possible to engage people doing unskilled, dreary, repetitive work? And is engagement an end in itself, or does it lead to other desirable outcomes such as productivity, profitability, staff retention, and customer satisfaction?

The research in this area shows pretty consistent findings. The results are neither surprising nor counterintuitive. And they have been known for ages. So why is it that supervisors and managers do not perform their duties so as to maximize the commitment and engagement of their staff?

There are some fairly basic but important things a manager needs to do to maximize engagement. They are presented here as a checklist, Management 101, a desiderata for the director / decision-maker / desktop.

- Let every person know what is expected of them in terms of their processes and products. Be clear. Check understandings. And revisit expectations as they change. All people have hopes and expectations about promotion, about change, about what their organization should be doing for them (and they for the organization). These expectations need to be managed.
- Give people the tools for the job. Keep them up to date. Train them to use these tools. Make sure that processes

are well thought through so that the technology people use is appropriate for what they are required to do. In short, give technical and informational support.

◆ Give people opportunities to learn and shine at what they are good at. People like to celebrate their skills, abilities, and unique gifts. Help them find and explore them. Let them do their best at all times. And encourage development of strengths.

◆ Be generous but targeted in praise. Recognize effort and success. Recognize individuals and how they strive to achieve. Celebrate success. Notice and praise individuals when they have put in extra effort. And do it openly, naturally, and regularly.

◆ Listen to your employees. They often have very good and innovative ideas. Yes, they can and do complain, but listen to that too. They need to believe their ideas count, their voice is heard, and they can contribute to how the work is arranged.

◆ Help them believe in the purpose or product of the organization. People need to feel their job is important; that they really are making a contribution to society. This involves more than writing fancy mission statements. It's about giving the job a sense of meaning and purpose.

◆ Encourage friendship formation at work. This is more than insisting on teamwork. It is giving people space and time to build up a friendship network. Friends are a major source of social support. They make all the difference to the working day. And committed people commit their friends.

◆ Talk to people about their progress. Give them a chance to let off steam, to dream about what might be, and to have quality time with you. This is more than those detailed, often rather forced appraisals. It is about opportunity for the boss to focus on the hopes, aspirations, and plans of the individual.

Pretty obvious stuff. Be clear about what you want. That is, define the outcomes required for individuals that will strengthen and challenge them. Focus on what they do well: their strengths, gifts, and talents. Try to find the best individual and the best in the individual. Make them exemplars, heroes, models. Find the right fit between a person's talents and ambitions and the tasks they need to do.

Look for ambitious, achievement-oriented, energetic individuals. But steer their striving: manage their route map. And look for, listen to, and reward evidence of independent ideas and thinking. Never assume management has a monopoly on the truth. Also encourage camaraderie: help people who are social animals relate to each other and pull together.

Do all of the above and you have an engaged workforce. And we do know that happy, healthy staff treat customers better. It's a relatively simple causal link. It pays to focus on staff engagement. But it's also the fundamental task of all management. Amen!

Marketing maladies

Marketers are the masters of the neologism. They, after all, invented *infotainment* and *advermation*. They babble on about *anticipointment* (the feeling you get when an event or campaign does not live up to the hype).

All seek *auditability* (withstanding auditor scrutiny) but are on the look out for *budgetunities* (innovative budgeting). Some become addicted to their *Crackberries* and the most unfortunate are *cryptonoids*, trying to read meanings into everything.

They talk of being *betamaxed* (when superior technology loses out) and describe colleagues as *cyberbeggars*, *cyberchondriacs*, *cyberskeptics*, and *cyberslackers*.

They *blameshift* at *blamestorming* meetings and enjoy *bobbleheading* agreement with senior managers. They like to be goal focused or *centergistic*, and try to *channelbalize* by stealing business from existing channels.

But they rarely turn the focus on themselves. They are both individually and en masse often rather odd. Outrageous disinhibited extroverts who started in sales as well as number tumbling, graph addicts from strategic planning. And, quite simply, many lose the plot. They suffer from delusions of grandeur, narcissistic personality disorder, even paranoia.

And there are problems to which they are particularly or uniquely prone as a result of their background and interest. The following dozen or so have recently been identified.

- *Tourette's BOGOF syndrome*: the irrational fear of shouting 'buy one, get one free' out loud in public places.

♦ *Delusional customer intimacy impulse*: the constant and bizarre belief that one could, or should, become intimate with customers in order to understand them better.

♦ *Chronic jingle tinnitus*: the result of listening to commercial radio to get their head around the marketing philosophy of their competitors.

♦ *Intermittent focus group dependency*: the now widely discredited belief that anything of note emerges when a manic facilitator encourages a group of vacuous and garrulous consumers to air their views.

♦ *Paranoid penetration phobia*: the inability to get into new markets successfully. Its opposite is idealized insertion impulse, which is the illogical need to place advertisements in places they should not go.

♦ *Adolescent market share fixation*: this is an obsessive compulsive spectrum disorder where patients believe that market share figures alone are meaningful and important.

♦ *Subliminal message syndrome*: this well-established illness stems from re-reading *The Hidden Persuaders*. It is the delusional belief that subliminal messages sell products.

♦ *Loss leader lethargy*: this is the result of wasting large sums of money on loss-leader ideas to get people into places where they might, but don't, buy anything else.

♦ *Bipolar qual/quant paralysis*: this is a new form of pedantic glossolalia where a person can't decide whether to do qualitative or quantitative research. It has a split-brain aspect to it.

♦ *Repetitive semiotics compulsion*: this originates in courses where people are alerted to the complex symbolism and meaning in signs. It can result in a catatonic state if the patient can read the *real* meaning into adverts.

♦ *Dysfunctional demographics dependency*: this is a most common problem, in which the patient started off analyzing simply by sex, age, and class, but now classifies all manner of daft, meaningless groups of customers using dodgy stats.

◆ *Award-seeking ad-prize obsession*: the belief that advertisements are successful at increasing sales or brand awareness if they win prizes at overrated, narcissistic festivals.

◆ *Blanket brandization illusion*: the belief that everything and everyone is a brand and that nebulous, vacuous, brandtalk helps people understand anything better.

Of course, diagnosis precedes cure, and marketing psychiatry is a young science. However, practitioners are aware that some of the above marketing maladies may prove particularly resistant to therapy.

Meeting mumbo-jumbo

Meetings frequently do, as the old adage has it, 'take minutes and waste hours.' Fully three-quarters or more of a senior manager's day may be taken up with meetings.

Despite deep cynicism about their productivity and usefulness, they remain sacrosanct. Many a caller has been fobbed off with the simple phrase 'He's in a meeting.' And woe betide the natural retort, 'Will you get him out of it because this is pretty damn important!'

Most of us know that meetings have little or nothing to do with the quality of decision-making or the communication of information. Their two major functions are, quite simply, diffusion of responsibility and decision acceptance. That is, they are there to ensure that all present take equal blame and responsibility for the decision (particularly if it goes wrong).

Frustration with the time-and-effort-wastefulness of meetings has led various organizations to attempt to implement certain strategies to improve them. Some follow a *structure*. Thus all meetings begin with *expectations* and end with *benefits* and *concerns*. Some try to shock with efficiency, calculating the ROI on all meetings by working out the real cost (in money) of them. This involves calculating the salaries of people present per hour and totaling it all up.

A recent fad is to color-code meetings beforehand to indicate the type and amount of acceptable and unacceptable behavior. Some like to follow the black- to red-alert categories used by police and security services. Others like a simple traffic-light system. But the trouble with both of these arrangements is that they bring conceptual associations. So a simple one-to-five with varied colors works best.

How does this work? Quite simple. It starts with some

criterion, like level of contribution or level of support. The color or number chosen for the meeting indicates the desired behavior. Thus a high number might indicate the expectation that everyone will chip in regularly; a low number means the meeting is more about receiving information.

This system is usually used for three types of issue. The first is about *process*, not *content*—that is, how attendees treat each other. In brainstorming there are very clear rules about no criticism of others' ideas, about valuing quantity over quality, about acceptable piggy-backing on somebody else's contributions. The same applies here.

Some process prescriptions are about politeness. Others are about simple things like how long one may speak for, or indeed how to get the floor in the first place. So a green meeting may indicate that what is required is short, crisp interjection. A blue meeting may indicate that it is acceptable to develop an idea.

Some meetings may prescribe, others proscribe, that humor is always a dangerous issue. Jokes can lighten the tone, but they can also offend. They may introduce inappropriate levity where seriousness is required. One useful rule is about criticism. A blue meeting may indicate no criticism; a green one criticism of certain features; yellow that no criticism is allowed unless a feasible alternative is apparent; and red that anything can be said.

More importantly the system can be applied to content. Thus the rule may be about rule-breaking—about really thinking outside the box, about radical reformation, not just adaptation. The color-indicated rules might put certain things out of bounds.

One of the advantages of this system is that it sets expectations beforehand. It's a bit like a dress code: black tie, smart casual, dress down. The rule says a lot about how the meeting is expected to go ... and therefore its outcome.

Meta-perception

Being perceptive is a competency, skill, and virtue at work. But it takes various forms: other, self, and meta-perception.

Some people are genuinely sensitive to the motives, needs, and peculiarities of others. Call it intuition or perspicacity, or whatever some people seem to have a lot more of it than others. All sorts of people need this skill: counselors, trainers, even politicians. It is about 'second guessing' people, knowing where they are coming from, perhaps even understanding others better than they understand themselves. And it may not be that easy to teach. It's part of what is now called emotional intelligence.

A second perception is self-perception—that is, a realistic appreciation of one's abilities, attractiveness, and general assets. There are many versions of inaccurate self-perception. Essentially these come in four forms: a genuine or faked over- or under-appreciation of one's ability or appeal. This, of course, ignores the possibility that people are totally accurate in their self-appraisal.

Some are deluded about their abilities, believing they are more talented than they are. They may be 'beneficiaries' of all that esteem-building nonsense which suggests that self-belief drives performance rather than the other way around.

Others may just bluff about their assets, particularly in job interviews, but have a fairly realistic appreciation of what they can and cannot do. Just as much as one finds inappropriate hubris, one finds inappropriate humility. This occurs when individuals underestimate their characteristics. They may believe they are less bright, less attractive, less creative, and less thin than they actually are. The latter problem is, of course, the main issue for anorexics. One can fake humility when it is culturally acceptable to do so.

Arrogance is often frowned upon ... and stamped upon. But genuine underestimation can lead to a self-fulfilling prophecy: underachievement. Underestimating oneself is about more than self-esteem and self-confidence. It is also about getting consistent and detailed feedback.

The third type of perception is most interesting. It's called meta-perception: your perception of their perception of you. Of course, you can have meta-meta-perception too: your perception of their perception of your perception of them.

Consider the world of work. What do those who work in finance think about themselves? That they are cautious, meticulous, and prudent custodians of the company assets. That they shrewdly and wisely control costs and protect profiles. But what do others think about them? Often that they are narrow-minded, obsessive bean counters with no vision and deeply risk averse. They are overly eager to control costs but they are a cost.

And what about those in production and engineering? They see themselves at the heart of the business because without the product there would be no business. They see themselves as hard-working, stoical, steady Eddie. Frequently harassed by sales, finance, HR, and marketing, who should be minding their own business.

But what do others think about them? Do they know? Do they care? Often they are seen as obsessive, obstructive, and obstreperous. They focus on deadlines, quality control, and raw materials—they are egocentric. Worse, they are ignorant and dismissive of the real needs of customers.

Not surprisingly, perhaps, all sections think they are at the centre of the business. Marketers believe that they, and they alone, understand the customer, see trends, plan ahead. They see themselves as courageous visionaries battling the entrenched conservatism of finance, production, and sales.

But others see them as costly star-gazers eager to have a good lunch, give away trinkets and toys, and spend, spend, spend. In fact, although marketers believe they are the ones 'in touch', many colleagues think they have lost the plot and are no close friends of reality. What they do is common sense, and they should be encouraged to do a day's hard and honest work every so often.

And HR? The people bit. They see themselves as the repository of interpersonal relations. They keep the show rolling. They do payroll and negotiation with the union, and selection and training. After all, people are our greatest asset, and we are the ones responsible for choosing and growing them. Nonsense. HR is peopled by form-obsessed, time wasters who have little understanding of the real business. They mistake form completion for management and are seriously prone to the fads and fashions of so-called business gurus. And there is little evidence that all that money spent on training has any beneficial effect.

So how good is departmental meta-perception? Does it matter? The answer is yes. We hear a great deal about 'silo' thinking and the need for communication, understanding, and integration.

The first thing to do in trying to break down stereotypes is to understand them. What do people think about you and why? Trainers and teachers need to be acutely good at meta-perception. They need to know, often on a minute-by-minute basis, how they are perceived.

But, alas, perception is only half the story. Even if one is good at all three, one needs to know how and when to change the behavior of others and, indeed, oneself. And that is at the heart of the emotional intelligence message that has echoed so strongly in business. We all need to be good at perceiving ourselves and others' emotions, and know how to change them.

Methods of payment

There is little to make the person running a small business feel more aggrieved, angry, and helpless than to have big, rich, powerful clients that delay payments. Cash-flow problems can lead to business failure.

How and when people pay their bills is an under-researched area. Why do some people pay in cash, others by check, and still others by standing order? Are cash buyers unsophisticated oldies or criminals trying to avoid detection? Are those fearful of using their credit cards paranoid inadequates? Are those who prefer standing orders (where appropriate) sensible citizens of the twenty-first century?

Also, how you pay can depend on many things: the size of the bill, the regularity of payment, the need for records being the primary factors. Some quaint customs like 'putting things on the slate' have practically disappeared. While paying on what older people quaintly call 'the never never' seems on the increase. There is sometimes limited choice for both those who invoice and those who pay. That is, your options are, of necessity, restricted. Both parties want safety and convenience ... and, of course, the cheapest way of paying in the long run.

There have, however, been some fascinating studies on methods of payment. One study looked at how psychological diagnosis differed according to method of payment. Nearly 200 American psychologists were sent the story of a fictitious patient, with clear symptoms of either anxiety or depression. The anxiety case gave all the symptoms to merit a clear diagnosis but the depressive case was less clear and there was no mention of the duration of the symptoms. Half were told they were to be paid by a managed care insurance policy and half that the fictitious patient would pay out of their own pocket. The task of the psychologists was to say whether they would assign a diagnosis and, if so, what it would be.

The results showed, first, that those who paid by managed care insurance were much more likely to receive a clear diagnosis. Furthermore the managed care group were more likely to be diagnosed by a catch-all 'adjustment disorder.' In fact, the anxious patients were ten times more likely to be diagnosed when the insurance paid than when they paid for themselves

One reason for this may be straightforward. Health care companies need an assigned diagnosis to justify and legitimate payment. And they may have been more likely to attribute an adjustment disorder because it is seen as less serious, or perhaps because this disorder category is very wide.

Another psychiatric study reported work where psychiatrists took delay in payment as an index of the progress of treatment. Thus if you saw your psychologist, say, once a week and were invoiced at the end of the month (for four sessions) and were paying yourself, the psychiatrist knew when the bills went out and when the check arrived. The more defensive or hostile or angry the person, the longer they took to pay. Certainly to withhold payment for shoddy, inadequate, or promise-unfulfilled work is not unusual, but this is all the more subtle.

Artisans have been known to charge people according to where they live, what vehicle they drive, and how much money they appear to have, as well as the nature of the job. And, of course, they want cash up front. Many fall for this only to pay later because they have no comeback with the fly-by-night builders who disappear into the shadows.

You don't often hear people asking, 'Is there a discount for cash?,' but you do hear questions about acceptability/

charges for credit or debit cards, Visa or American Express. Some are not accepted by retailers because of charges, or payment delay, or whatever. Hotels demand a credit card imprint as guarantee ... or alternatively an outrageous sum of cash 'to cover petty items.'

And we have seen in some places the re-emergence of bartering. In a way, the middle class have always done this through their connections. Through college, workplace, and club connections they have made contact with all the (expensive) professionals they are ever likely to need: doctor and dentist, accountant and lawyer, psychologist and journalist. And reciprocal help is proffered and received.

Alas, nice middle-class professionals probably don't know too many electricians or plumbers, car mechanics, or house decorators. So there may be a serious class divide in the 'bartering syndicate.' It's usually as much about convenience and trust as costs and tax dodging.

But it remains a fact: how and when people pay for goods and services says much about them. Stores, banks, and other financial institutions know this. Hence the exclusivity of the gold card, and the advantage of the privileged preview.

Equally, but less obviously, how we charge may be more influenced than we realize by how we pay. It's a field day for ethicists as we see all sorts of respectable people happy, even proud, to boast of 'ripping off' big institutions by overcharging—something they would be less likely do to individuals and never to friends.

Morning prayers and evening vespers

In most big organizations the 'top team' (the board, the grown-ups) meet either daily, or minimally once a week, to steer the ship, agree plans, and run the show.

Where and when they meet are part of the tradition, often dictated by the preferences and whims of an earlier CEO. His or her chronobiology (read morning or evening type preferences) probably played a large part in that choice.

Some organizations have morning prayers. And that is what they are called. Usually every Monday, probably every Friday, and occasionally every Wednesday, the grown-ups turn up in the plush boardroom with its oval table to do the business. The British might start at 10 AM, the Germans at 9 AM, and the Americans at 8 AM.

These meetings have a pattern: norms develop, the formal and informal agenda. This includes what is discussed, when, and how, as well as the usual length of the meeting. There's the brisk-with-no-break version, the coffee-with-posh-Danish version, and the (now very rare) damn-good-lunch version.

While morning prayers are common, some organizations have inherited the evening vespers model. This is a mid- to late-afternoon time slot (4 PM-ish). These too vary in history and pace. Some end rather nicely with claret and tapas … and gossip. Others terminate more with a whimper than a bang.

What are the psychological differences and consequences of having a morning versus an evening meeting? Given that the fundamental task is the same there should be little difference. But of course there is. The feel, the tone, and also the process may be strikingly different according to the time of day.

Morning meetings tend to be brisker and more businesslike. Banter and small talk go faster. One obvious reason for this is the domino effect of being late for subsequent appointments. Most senior people have packed diaries. They move from one meeting to another with bewildering regularity. And seniority means their meetings may revolve around them. So if they are not present things cannot or do not happen.

Morning meetings not only have tighter schedules but they often feel quite different. They are at the beginning of the day. Things seem to be ahead of one and this can spill over to the agenda. The briefing at breakfast time may be a 1980s thing but its psychology is simple. First thing means *important*. Larks, but not owls, are fresh, attentive, on-the-ball at the beginning of the day.

Vespers is very different. Few have business events after the meeting, though there may be some charity event. This means less rush. People may be more tired or just more sanguine at the end of the day. They may also be more hungry.

With fewer time constraints these meetings last longer. They may easily run into domestic time. Snacks may be served. Indeed, they may often establish a normative pattern of looking like a cocktail party after 6.30PM.

Ask people which they would prefer and you will get different responses. The PC, grown-up, serious director answer is probably morning payers. But most confess a love of vespers. Evenings meetings are more likely to include gossip, which improves organizational communication and cements relationships.

An agreement to Chatham House Rules and a tasty nibble on a weekly basis can do a lot to help grown-ups understand and appreciate each other. Some may even enjoy the excuse not to rush home. Dare one venture to say that these people are more likely to be men? Indeed, work–life balancers may rather resent the concept of vespers.

Muzak while you spend

The best predictor of how much money you spend in a store is how long you spend there. Not your wealth, your shopping intentions, your gender, or even your shopaholic or shopaphobic tendencies: quite simply, time spent = money spent.

So how to keep you there? Disorient you with maze-like passages. Mirrors to slow you down while you inspect your tie or make-up.

And they play muzak. It has been argued, rather than proven, that department store customers exposed to muzak shop for about 20 percent longer than when there is no muzak, and also spend about a fifth more money. Why? Perhaps because the music relaxes them, or puts them in a better mood. Music is a good drug: legal, non-addictive, and very fast working.

Commercial organizations have not been slow to see the financial rewards of using music in stores, restaurants, banks, and so on, and there is now a fascinating and significant body of literature on the topic, spearheaded by the UK's Adrian North and his colleagues at Leicester University's psychology department. Their studies have been imaginative and revealing.

In one they agreed with a supermarket to play either stereotypically French or German music on alternate days for a fortnight in the part of the store selling wine. They measured the amount and type of wine bought in this period. Yes, it worked! French music led to more sales of French wine and German music to a preference for German wine. Interestingly, when questioned, customers were unaware of the music and its potential effects on their product choice. Not quite subliminal selling, but not far from it.

In a similar study either classical, pop, or no music at all was played in a British restaurant over the course of nearly three weeks. Researchers measured time and money spent, the latter being broken down between drink and food. The customers spent more time and money (on starters and coffee, but not booze) when the classical music was playing. The researchers offered three explanations for these potentially important findings: classical music was synergistic with all other aspects of the restaurant atmosphere. Second, the patrons simply preferred it and transferred their good response to increased time and money spent. The third explanation was that classical music promotes an upscale atmosphere in which it is natural to spend more money. Of course, all explanations could apply simultaneously.

What about other settings? In another study researchers played classical, 'easy listening,' or no music in a bank and a bar, and customers were asked to rate the overall atmosphere of the two places. The more they liked the music the better they evaluated the atmosphere on three dimensions, and the more they were prepared to pay for products on sale in the bar. But other things also made a difference; these included the volume of the music and the time of day. However much one likes certain music there is clearly an optimal level.

And what about the potential of music to influence our perception of time? This factor has not escaped our resourceful researchers. In another study they kept callers waiting on the phone, playing them either a selection of songs by The Beatles (either in their original form or a pan-pipe version) or one of those 'please hold, the line is busy, you are in a queue …' messages repeated every ten seconds. They measured how long people were prepared to hold and also their liking for the music played. The pan pipes came out top. People were prepared to hold longer with music they liked: over a minute longer than the 'sorry caller' repeat. On-hold music affects holding on!

Presumably music could be used to 'move people on' as much as it can serve to keep them in an environment.

Music and muzak condition environments. They change the mood and then the behavior of customers in those settings. And people are not always aware of the music unless it is too loud or, for them, particularly unpleasant. Music can influence time and money spent in small but predictable and significant ways.

Non-executive directors

Wise, disinterested, and business savvy; or political, powerless, and prying? Which is more true of the non-executive director (NEO)? Who volunteers and who is chosen as NEO?

They certainly come in different shapes and sizes. Most come from, and go to, the private sector, but more and more often they are welcomed by the public sector to bring a little of their entrepreneurial flair. Occasionally, public-sector-trained NEOs go to the private sector, but the journey is predominantly in the other direction.

Why have NEOs on the board? What difference do they make? Are there demonstrable benefits to having them? And, if so, where do you find them?

Many will attest to the enormous value of a good NEO. Their very status as inside-outsiders means that they can ask really challenging questions. They are allowed to think the unthinkable, question the taboos, confront the demons.

Boards can be prone to groupthink, particularly when they are going through a protracted period of crisis, but also in times of success. The signs of groupthink are well known: collective rationalization, illusions of unanimity, strong conformity, pressure, and even mind-guards who are the 'whips' of the board. In good times they can experience illusions of invulnerability by ignoring danger signals, taking risks and being naively over-optimistic. In bad times they exhibit excessive negative stereotyping of opponents and an unquestioning morality about their position.

Boards with groupthink don't evaluate alternatives and risks well. And they eschew advice from anyone not in the inner circle. And this is where the NEO can be most helpful. They can be devil's advocate, philosophic logician, or naive questioner. They may indeed have both expertise and experience in particular areas that the board lacks.

They may also play another type of counseling role. The board is supposed to consist of grown-ups, though their petty jealousies, unstable temperaments, and overwhelming ambitions may cause meetings to resemble kindergartens.

NEOs can be process consultants trying to understand and improve the relationship between directors. They can arbitrate, reflect back, and counsel. Their role may therefore be as much psychological as strategic.

NEOs may be asked to make certain decisions the board feels it cannot or should not. It is they who may decide on the pay rises of board members. They may even play a major part in deciding who joins and who leaves the board.

So who are these benevolent oracular gurus who volunteer for the job? Many are called but few are chosen. Many NEOs are semi-retired successful business people. They have made their pile, worked hard, and are still young, fit and interested. Even in their late forties, but more like their late fifties, they like a few days a week or a month as an arrangement.

Having two or three NEOs 'on the go' is a nice little earner and an amusement for some individuals. It is interesting work and can be very well remunerated. There is no shortage of people queuing up for such roles.

It is tempting to get 'a friend' in one sense or another on the board. People from one's own background and sector, sharing similar socio-political beliefs, may be easy to get on with but not challenging enough. You get most value from a NEO who is clever and with wide business experience; from someone who is courageous to challenge yet judicious in his/her counseling skills.

You don't get as much value from a moderately bored ex-executive who is a personal friend of the chairman and likes exercising his or her power.

Organizational amnesia

When you succeed nobody remembers, but when you fail nobody forgets. We know much about personal forgetting and forgetfulness, but what of organizational forgetting? What of the organization that seems to record nothing but repeated failed initiatives again and again?

People forget for many reasons: they may suppress memories or they may suffer illness or brain damage that quite simply destroys the stores of knowledge. It is terrifying for the individual and immensely sad to witness in those we know. And trauma can trigger amnesia or other fascinating psychiatric states such as hysterical fugue.

But how, when, and why do organizations forget or lose knowledge? This partly depends on how and where those memories are stored. Knowledge and information are often stored in procedures, rules, and routines. Standard operating procedures are (usually) based on knowledge. They are, or should be, partly the result of the experience of the organization. What works and why? When and how? They should result from both theory and trial and error, experimentation and feedback. But routinization can lead to stagnation. Old learning, redundant processes, out-of-date evidence-free procedures remain and can be passionately defended even though the reason they exist is forgotten. Bureaucracies may be particularly and pathologically prone to remembering where forgetfulness may actually be an asset.

Is it therefore always a sign of failure, even disaster, to forget? Could it not be that, just as with individuals, forgetting can be adaptive? Some organizational forgetting may be really helpful. Erasing the tape, throwing out the old technology, allows (literally and metaphorically) more space for the new stuff. In this way forgetting may have to precede learning. Forgetting is thus positive: it is unlearning that which inhibits progress. Old learning can really inhibit the assimilation of new knowledge.

Organizational amnesia can be caused by trauma or incompetence. But it probably remains useful to see it as either accidental or purposeful—that is, unplanned and undesirable, or planned and deliberate. Furthermore, what is forgotten is important: is it old, established knowledge, or new knowledge?

Thus we can have different possibilities. *First*, forgetting what we know, when this information is useful and has not been supplanted. This is the accidental, inefficient loss, deterioration, or distortion of established knowledge. How does that happen? Partly through lack of practice. Partly when critical people leave (en masse). It is really bad news for the organization and can lead to very quick disintegration.

Second, there is the deliberate attempt to forget. To purge the past. To airbrush out of history individuals, events, and procedures that do not suit the present. This is managed unlearning. It can be dramatic, draconian, and disastrous, but it can be successful. When old institutions have to reinvent themselves, they need a new everything: badge, motto, uniform, and procedures. All the old ways need to be replaced with a clean sweep. Best forgotten. Best not alluded to. The past is, and should be, another country. You need not, must not, should not, go there. It has too much 'stuff' to deal with. So we conspire to forget. Not distort. Not rewrite. But start again. Year zero, as per Pol Pot.

Third, there is the failure to consolidate, retain, or use new knowledge. Somehow (good) new ideas do not get translated into routines or practices. Useful learning from critical issues never makes it to the collective consciousness of organizations. The new knowledge may be retained for a short period but it is never embedded and hence retained. How does this occur? It could be that nobody knew how to codify that knowledge. Or nobody really knew whose responsibility it was. Or that it was met with initial resistance. Or that nobody realized the long-term implications and necessity of implementing the new knowledge in new procedures. But it is a sure sign of failure for the organization. It means it cannot really learn.

Fourth, there is the forgetting of the new: abandoning innovations or giving up on new ideas. This can be both functional and dysfunctional. It can mean the introduction of a new system that, for whatever reason, does not work: unreliable, inappropriate, over-complex, or before its time. Interesting organizations that are innovative (through trial and error) have to be quite good at forgetting. They need to have a go, try the novel, and, if not a good idea, move on, wipe the slate clean, and begin again. But it's dysfunctional if new knowledge is forgotten before it has really had time to be digested or tested. This is a result of staff resistance, a fear of the new or a dislike of innovation. In this instance it can be seriously problematic.

The moral? If knowledge is power, if knowledgeable workers are the key, then knowledge storage is pretty important. This is more than a filing system. It is the short-term memory of the organization. It's a critical element in the intelligence of that organization. We cannot really talk of organizational learning without all those concepts like storage and memory. And key to understanding how we don't forget is why we do forget.

To forgive and forget is a virtue. To fail to recall critical events and procedures can be a disaster. An organization needs to prevent as much as possible new useful knowledge being forgotten, but encourage the letting go of old, redundant processes and procedures. Forgetting may be part of unlearning, which is crucial to incorporating new learning and new knowledge.

So, under some circumstances, amnesia is really good for the organization. In others it is a disaster. What is important is to remember the difference.

Organizational death

Dust to bust, cashes to ashes. Like individuals, organizations die. Firms go bust; companies have to call in the receiver; stores, restaurants, and consultancies fail and go out of business. Public-sector departments and whole organizations are closed down. They might be inefficient, ineffective, out-of-date, redundant, or simply a victim of cuts. And their demise can easily cause as much pain, anguish, and poverty as the death of an individual. Late-middle-aged redundant workers can feel as disoriented, grief-stricken, and bewildered as if they had lost their spouses.

Some, of course, are pleased to see the whole shebang fold up. Just as there may be relief in saying goodbye to a fickle, demanding, and difficult relative, so there may be (secret) pleasure in seeing the doors closed for the last time. Good riddance ... and all that.

All cultures mark the passing of the dead. They know that the grief process and the healing of the bereaved is greatly helped by rites, rituals, and ceremonies. Burials, funerals, and a 'celebration of the life lived' all help. So why not bury an organization? Why not have a proper ceremony to acknowledge the event?

What is the function of the funeral or life-celebration event? There are probably many functions—all slightly different but all significant.

◈ Funerals help articulate the pain of the grieving. They can and should articulate and evoke the deeply felt, albeit incoherent, emotions of survival. Well-chosen words can bring people together, speak for them, ease their pain.

- Equally, funerals can, by being called 'celebrations of a life,' be a sensible and sensitive counterweight to grief. The service rejoices in the successes of the past. It uses humor to drive out the gloom. It does the 'warts and all' to pinch one back to reality.
- A good funeral always insists that the person in some sense survives death. There is psychological or spiritual, if not physical, survival. The person survives in those whom they touch and in that which they made. There is life after death.
- Funerals can also admit the despair of the doubter and the anguish of the atheist. They can admit that all might have been in vain.
- A funeral can remind one of a legacy. Children and relatives, past pupils, and friends, as well as works of invention are testimony to the fact that there is always a legacy.
- Death is a natural part of life. It is part of the cycle. Letting go happens. And funerals normalize the process.

To deny that the collapse of an organization is deeply traumatic is to be blind to the real psychological function of work. Yes, work is primarily a source of income but it is also a source of identity, of purpose, of friends, and of structure. Many become temporarily bewildered after retirement. They experience anomie, alienation, and loss.

It can certainly help the grieving and adaptation process to have a good send-off. Some people need consolation, others thanks. They like to know that their years of toil were not pointless. They like the idea of some legacy.

So when the plant closes or the business folds it may be kind and helpful to have a wake. Call it what you will: a memorial drinks party or a thanksgiving.

Personal risk assessment

It's only in very particular jobs that assessment seems to involve selecting out, rather than selecting in. People with access to arms, large sums of money, or secrets of the business or state variety seem scrutinized more carefully than others.

There are those who, therefore, specialize in personal risk assessment. They have to be psychologically minded and they have to be perceptive. It is their job to look for certain 'markers' or predictors of problems such as breakdown, derailment, or dishonesty.

One of the great mysteries and paradoxes of the selection world is that there is no correlation between job level and person scrutiny. Indeed, the relationship seems very negative—that is, HR people seem to spend more money and effort on the likes of graduate trainees than the CEO; no one would dare give a prospective CEO an intelligence test or do any serious CV checking.

So resources are spent on those who are just starting out and relatively junior, while much less is spent on those that can do real damage because of their seniority, budget, or access to information.

If you are in the business of personal risk management or selecting out, what should you look out for? There are probably around six traits or syndromes worth spotting. They are all well known to clinicians, though they might use rather different language. Each issue deserve serious consideration and perceptive questioning.

1. *Relationships*: this may be a real can of worms, but it is very diagnostic. It extends from relationships with

parents in childhood, to those with authority figures (as well as adult partners and spouses, and of course people at work). Some people may be rather dependent on others, some very solitary, but the major issue concerns forming and maintaining *any* social relationship. They may be excessively shy or bold but probably very low on EQ, empathy, and engagement. This must be bad news: the higher you go in business, the more it is actually all about relationships. Does the individual have healthy, happy, long-term relationships?

2. *Impulsivity and immaturity*: again, this has many manifestations. One sign is that such people are easily bored and poor at self-control. Adult ADHD may or may not be a clinical syndrome. The impulsivity issue concerns instant gratification, little planning, and self-indulgence. The immaturity is about prototypical teenager behavior: fragile, oversensitive, restless, moody—moving from arrogant cockiness to demoralized helplessness in minutes. They are also nearly always self-indulgent.

3. *Machiavellianism and manipulativeness*: beware the rebellious charmer who pays little attention to rules and regulations. If both bright and good-looking, their seductive charm can make them lethal. They can be superficial, glib, flippant, and inconsistent, but they are also all things to all people. They are often amoral and immoral, and deeply indifferent to the feelings and needs of others.

4. *Angry, resentful, and negative oriented*: there are many forms of negativity. There are the 'passed over and pissed off,' those with a generally negative world-view. There are the passive-aggressive and those who see doom and gloom everywhere. Most are in the blame game for all their misfortunes. They see the world as unjust and often feel victims on many levels. They report a history of negativity.

5. *Extremes of self-belief:* psychologists have hundreds of self-words, from self-actualization through self-esteem to self-handicapping strategies. Self-awareness is a key indicator of mental health and adjustment. Some problem people have a strange self-image and issues around self-esteem. Some try to cover up low self-esteem with grandiose overcompensation. Some have succumbed to self-aggrandizing therapy, which equates delusions of grandeur with mental health. Know thyself. To thy own self be true. Indeed. Much is to be gained, therefore, from references as opposed to inter-views, and particularly from the disparity between the two.

6. *Inflexibility, rigidity, obsessionality:* beware the over-dutiful and diligent, the over-cautious and over-careful. Rigid people are deeply change averse and often strictly routinized. They are made fearful and nervous unless everything is clear, orderly, and predictable—but alas it never can be. They are intolerant of ambiguity and avoid uncertainty. They can easily become fetishistic about the oddest things.

The above checklist is a sort of 'six of the worst.' But be careful not to look only for attributes you want in people while turning a blind eye to those you don't. Love, they say, is blind—perhaps that is why nearly half of all marriages fail. Make sure you aren't blinded to candidates' faults in the selection process.

Personality and income

Organizational psychologists have long argued that personality traits predict success at work. Stable, conscientious, bright people do better, particularly in more complex jobs. Whether you 'believe in' the validity, usefulness, and fairness of psychometric tests of personality and ability or not, everyone looks for personality characteristics at the selection interview. It is just common sense.

So if traits predict success at work they should also predict income among adults.

And this is precisely what a study in the *Journal of Economic Psychology* (June, 2005) set out to test. A Norwegian and a Spanish economist used Dutch data to test a theory. The theory suggests that there are established, robust, and replicable personality trait predictors of income *over and above* education.

There are wage-related rewards for certain psychological variables in the labor market. In other words, employers pay more for certain individual characteristics. We know that beauty, height, obesity, and personal cleanliness are robust predictors of earnings. These may be related in part to personality factors like self-control and conscientiousness.

Personality traits are rewarded and punished in any labor market over and above human capital and job-specific training variables. Personality describes typical behaviors, preferences, and predictions. Thus extroverts seek out people for stimulation while over-aroused introverts tend to prefer their own company. Neurotics are prone to depression and seem to have free-floating anxiety. They are easily upset and moody, and often have a history of hypochondria.

Personality traits are stable over time. An extrovert at 12 is going to be an extrovert at 65, though perhaps a little less rowdy. Even with therapy, counseling, and cognitive behavior therapy, the unstable child is likely to grow into the sensitive adult. It's hard-wired.

But precisely which traits predict income, and why? The researchers found that *emotional stability* is strongly and positively associated with the income of both men and women. No surprise there: low scores on stability imply neuroticism (or negative affectivity, if you prefer). Neurotics are stress prone, pessimistic, and volatile. They are unlikely to be promoted to senior positions and, if they are, often crack under the strain. You need hardy, steady people at the helm and they are well rewarded for it.

Agreeableness, as a trait, was significantly associated with lower salaries among women. Agreeable people are kind, warm, empathic, and selfless. They are attracted to jobs that involve caring for others. And these are not well paid. The relationship is less strong in men, but in the same direction. Well-paid jobs call for toughness: making hard decisions; 'kicking ass,' as it's put in America. The too agreeable are too forgiving, and too lenient.

Interestingly, *conscientiousness*—that trait associated with diligence, dutifulness, and hard work—tends to be rewarded only at the beginning of an employment period. As one climbs the greasy pole, it seems that other factors become important. Or it may be that, once employed, conscientious workers work hard but without extra pay.

Being either an introvert or an extrovert had little impact, but *autonomy* did. This is the propensity to make personal decisions, and exert a degree of initiative and control. This was important in men.

What the study found was that, although personality factors were important, they interacted with other variables like gender, education, and amount of work experience. They were important on their own and in interaction with other factors.

The researchers suggest that schools promote personality traits that are rewarded in the labor market, like learning to control emotions and being more independent. They are, however, clear that the opposite of agreeableness is Machiavellianism, and that is definitely not so attractive in the workplace.

JOCKS, LONERS, DRUGGIES, AND NERDS

The British Government appears at last to have woken up to the fact that high numbers of its citizens are floating (pretty precariously) on a sea of debt. Many of them have little, if anything, saved, and, worse, have credit card and other debts they do not seem able to pay off.

Whence this dilemma? Is this a function of the policies of a dour and supposedly prudent Chancellor, who appears to prefer free spending to saving? Has he created an illusion of a successful economy, which will go wrong once the credit boom stops? Or have we become, over the years, a nation of spendthrifts—unwilling, unable, or unresponsive to saving? Why bother about a rainy day: the state will provide. Live for the moment: we do not know what tomorrow may bring.

All parents want their children to grow up money-savvy. They want them to understand money and use it wisely. They don't want misers or spendthrifts, gamblers or godfathers in the family. They want their children to be money-rational. And so they introduce pocket money or allowance regimes at an early age to teach them about finance.

There remains some debate about when pocket money should begin and the rules that you might apply: start around the age of five; pay once a week, moving on to once a month when they become adolescents; agree clear rules about what the money is for; encourage saving.

And you might teach them about the world of work through the time-honored weekend job or the paper round, or a stint as a waiter/waitress. It's good for their social, moral, and economic development. It is how they are integrated into society and learn to become upstanding, responsible citizens.

But all parents know and dread the power of the peer group. They worry about their children falling among thieves; about getting in with the wrong crowd; about being inappropriately socialized by ne'er-do-wells who become no-hopers.

We know that binge drinking and drug abuse in young people is heavily influenced by peer groups. But what about economic behavior such as saving money?

A recent Canadian study published in the *Journal of Economic Psychology* looked at the effects of peer groups and the experience of work on young (aged 12–24 years) people's saving behavior. The researchers were able to describe four clear youth subcultures. First, there is the fun, somewhat *delinquent*, subculture of hedonists. They are populated by 'druggies and partiers.' Opposite them are those in a *studious, academic* subculture. They enjoy school, work hard, and have a rich extra-curricular set of activities. They have been called 'brains' and 'nerds,' depending on your values.

A third group is populated by 'loners and nobodies.' They are *uninvolved, non-groupies*. They are not part of teen culture and little involved in any groups. They may not be influenced by others very much but can appear rather lost, inconspicuous outsiders who don't get accepted.

Finally, the '*jocks and populars*' come from the play-hard, work-hard, well-rounded culture that is both peer oriented and adult (achievement) oriented.

These subcultures dictate how young people speak, dress, spend, and play. They relate to all aspects of their lives—from how hard they try at school, to whether they take on part-time jobs, and how they spend and save their money.

The results of the study confirmed the researchers' hypotheses. So the 'brains' and 'populars' (nerds and jocks) saved, while the 'partiers' and 'loners' did not. Those more conscious of the adult world (the formal reward systems from school and work) saved more than those who paid more attention to the peer-oriented world (the informal reward system of short-term fun and acceptance).

Interestingly, those young people who worked were more saving oriented than those who did not. Sure, they had more money to save, but the results suggest they sought jobs in order to save.

It comes as no surprise that youth culture powerfully affects young people's attitudes towards, and use (or abuse) of money. Being a member of a group affects their reputation and their normative behavior. They are usually highly sensitive to how their peers behave, and gain acceptance from emulating this.

The young people who, through their parents' and teachers' encouragement, or through their own choice, become deeply involved in extra-curricular activities such as team sports, book clubs, or the performing arts soon begin to develop a more adult outlook with adult responsibilities. And that includes being sensible with money. So all the good work put in over a long period with pocket money advocators can easily be undone by feckless, hedonistic, peer group pressure. Equally the carefree, feckless young person can, with the right peers, learn to become a grown-up quite quickly, and be eminently sensible with their money.

Pester power

Pester power is a new name for an old concept. It is a favorite topic for conspiracy theorists, anti-capitalists, and consumer boycotters.

The 'theory' goes like this. There is a new chain of command in shopping. Retailers, advertisers, and manufacturers have learnt how to target your wallet, via your children. Through advertising, astute supermarket-based product placement, and deals with schools, young people are deliberately and cynically targeted.

Young people—children and adolescents—are naive and easily hoodwinked by clever advertising. They are gullible, believing all they see and hear, and are easily persuaded that they must have various products (toys, candy, and so on). The child then pesters the parent to buy the products. The exhausted and intimidated parent soon gives in and buys the product.

This then leads to a vicious cycle. Part of the cost of the product is spent in advertising, which increases pester power, which wears down parents more, leading them to buy more and more things they either can't afford or believe to be bad for their children.

So we read that supermarkets place certain goods—expensive breakfast cereals (with collectables), toys, and candy—at eye level in the aisle and at checkouts to maximize pester power. Some parents, it seems, have ceded household decision-making to children. Children influence parents' choice of cars, cell phones, electronics, and fashion items, so are targeted by manufacturers.

A few products are the major focus of the pester-power story: toys, fizzy drinks, and confectionery. And various health lobbyists see an entry point. They believe ordinary families find advertising is distorting their healthy eating patterns. Parents, it is said, feel powerless to counteract advertising that pushes junk food towards them.

In fact, all the above are myths, as careful disinterested research has shown. But the conspiracy theory lobby wants legislation: ban advertisements aimed at children; ban advertisements and product placement in schools; insist that all packaging lists contents and that media product placement in programs be strongly controlled; insist all organizations publicize who did market research and advertisement creation for all ads aimed at children; publish a Parents' Bill of Rights, and strictly enforce it.

The pester-power model takes the form of a causal chain: advertisements cause wants, which lead to demands, and then child–parent conflict, and then reluctant purchase by parent. But there are various other, better, evidence-based models.

Another more comprehensive model goes like this. Parents' lifestyle, values, and rules influence factors such as how much television children watch, their peer (friendship) group, and their personal preferences. These factors also determine how much pocket money children get and the rules that go with it.

Some parents attempt, wisely, to make their children media and shopping literate. By making it fun and interesting they educate their children on shopping trips. They discuss why they choose one product over another. It may be cost, freshness, country of origin, or fat content. At home they talk about the ads—the motives of the advertiser, the qualities of the product.

The facts quite plainly are these. What determines a young person's demands/requests for and use of all manner of products—such as alcopops, fast food, and the like—is essentially parenting style, then the child's peer group, then the child's personality and ability, then their media consumption, and, finally, their disposable income.

A major problem with the argument for legislation is that it erroneously supposes and overemphasizes children's naivety and gullibility and then, even worse, increases this infantilization by discouraging their access to the commercial world.

The Internet, of course, is feared by dictators and legislators alike. Pre-school children have access to computers and many primary school children are proficient at surfing the web.

The solution to pester power is never going to be preventing advertising or closing down fast-food chains. The solution lies in education: first parents, then children. Shop together, eat together, watch TV together, and discuss what you are doing. Criticize products you do not approve of, but give good reasons. Have rules about pocket money, treats, media consumption, and friends.

And if that doesn't work, a bit of parental assertiveness training would be a worthwhile investment.

Pluralistic ignorance

This concept refers to people holding back from publicly stating a view because they believe others feel differently. The lack of shared information then sustains a false impression.

Consider the following typical situation. Three couples try to meet up for a social event—say dinner and a trip to the theater. Business and family commitments lead to many cancellations, but eventually all can make it. Alas the meal is mediocre and the show a flop. It has taken a lot of effort and money to arrange the evening. So in order not to dampen morale and deter future possible events they all end the evening publicly saying how good the food was and how enchanting the play. To an outsider it looks like a great success. But once each couple is in the car, alone, they soon confess their real reactions. The evening was an expensive flop.

Another classic example comes from an early study on attitudes toward defense and disarmament among a national sample of voters. Results showed that, personally, 70 percent of these respondents favored disarmament, even if it meant loss of income. However, only 38 percent of them thought that others felt that way. Therefore, the dominant view supported disarmament but it was not perceived thus.

Another example concerns what people said they intended to do with money received from income tax cuts. A poll conducted by telephone asked a national sample: 'If you received a tax cut, would you spend most of it or save most of it?' They were also asked: 'Do you think most people would spend more than they would save, or save more than they would spend?' Over half (53 percent) said they would save more, but believed less than a quarter (22 percent) would do likewise. Similarly, only a third (33 percent) said they would spend more, while believing two-thirds (66 percent) would do so. Evidently, individuals intended to save their money in a considerably higher proportion than they believed others would. But, if those others are like themselves, the belief is greatly mistaken.

How does pluralistic ignorance operate in the office? Most of us feel constrained by a number of forces, from political correctness to threat of dismissal, in not saying what we think about a whole range of issues. Indeed, we are often compelled to say the opposite, thus ensuring pluralistic ignorance.

The results of climate surveys and 360-degree feedback can break the circle of ignorance. If, and only if, the respondent feels completely confident that their response really is anonymous do they feel secure enough to say what they think. Hence the shock for senior managers who, after years of biased feedback, get the truth of how others see them. The usual way of getting feedback, through open appraisals and the like, can encourage pluralistic ignorance. This is more frequently the case in secretive, non-communicative organizations, where employees really have no idea what their colleagues truly think.

The shrewd manager can really exploit this phenomenon. If no one dares say they feel underpaid, neglected, abused, badly managed, or whatever, a new (or even long-standing) employee may feel they are the odd one out, they have strange perceptions, they are not normal. These managers may have discovered that any survey or attempt to find out (and dare publish) what the workforce really thinks opens up a can of worms. It empowers staff, unites them, and builds a sense of community—often in opposition to the bad boss. So pluralistic ignorance can be bliss for the weak manager.

The whole business of pluralistic ignorance is a real worry for market researchers. It can lead their predictions to be terribly wrong. And it can yield odd effects when people are poorly informed about what other people really do or think. What are people's real beliefs about both corporate and capital punishment? What do they really think about abortion or adultery? How will they vote in the next election?

All believe they are above average in intelligence. All believe they are safer drivers than the next person. And by definition they are wrong.

But perhaps it is the problem of political correctness that has really stimulated pluralistic ignorance. People hold views about many issues they feel inhibited talking about. Sex, race, religion, disability, education … the PC police are everywhere. For some it is like having the eyes of the Stasi on them at every turn. So they express the PC view while actually holding a different view. And when they can be assured anonymity and confidentiality—at the ballot box, say—they let people know what they really think. This can cause very big surprises and wreck predictions. The price of political correctness may be pluralistic ignorance.

Prioritizing the Priory

Statistics on addiction in the workplace are often conflicting and unreliable. Some lobby groups want them to be high; others low. Thus those who want to raise the issue of stress in the workplace, or who are anti-drink, are eager to 'expose the truth' about alcohol and drug abuse at all levels in organizations. Others are happy to note the fact that they reside in a smoke- and alcohol-free building. Others have a vested interest in covering up the incidence of abuse. They include senior management, drinks companies, even shareholders.

So it becomes difficult to know if addictions are on the rise or in decline. Or indeed both at the same time, but different in different sectors, and with people at different levels.

Alcohol is an old drug. Nearly every culture has discovered alcohol and has pre- and proscribed many sorts of behaviors associated with it. Some cultures, like Jewish people, are restrained with alcohol and show low incidence of abuse. The Nordic peoples are the opposite.

And cultural norms are changing. The boozy business lunch is a thing of the past for most people. Even a couple of pints and a bar meal are now frowned upon by both the health and productivity lobbies. Some organizations are completely dry: booze and boozing is banned in all buildings. Some discreetly have accounts at famous treatment centers, like The Priory in the UK or the Betty Ford Center in the US, without dealing with or thinking about the real issues.

But what do we know about alcohol abuse? And what can we do about it? And why are some professions—cooks, journalists, diplomats, and politicians—over-represented in the statistics?

What defines an alcoholic? What separates the heavy drinker, the social drinker, the binge drinker, and the alcoholic? Alas the line is rather blurred, even to the sober. Three factors seem to determine whether the line is crossed. They refer to *quantity, frequency,* and *motivation* for drinking. Certainly it is difficult to imagine that consuming a bottle or more of spirits a day does not lead one to qualify. A bottle of wine a day is also a potential problem. That's 50 units of alcohol a week: twice the recommended intake for men.

But quantity does not take into consideration body weight, age, or metabolic system. Older, heavier people can hold their drink better: it takes more to get them intoxicated. But there is no clear cut-off point. There are green, amber, pink, red, and bright-red zones.

Frequency of drinking is also an issue. This refers to time of day as well as whether drinking is binge or session-like. We all know that a person who drinks early in the day has a problem. We know that people who stay blind drunk all weekend or right through their vacation have a problem. If you listen to the 'experts' the average middle-class dinner party is a binge-drinking session.

But where, what, and how frequently you drink does have important implications for health. The very definition of addiction is that you require regular 'top-ups.' It becomes an abiding passion to find the source of the next fix. Everyday drinking could be a sign.

Another more complicated issue is *why* people drink. Drink is a paradoxical stimulant: it is a physical depressant but a social stimulant. It gives people Dutch courage. It can help to get parties going. It is an effective lubricant. But it also helps one come down quickly after tension. So the time-deadlined professions (cooks, journalists), and the emergency professions (doctors, fire-fighters) are prone to finding it just too much of a crutch. And then there are those professions that float on a sea of socially prescribed alcohol. Diplomats, bar owners, brewers, and distillers are prone to problems.

Difficulties arise when people find they can perform well (or so they think) only with a couple of stiff drinks inside them. They have learnt to become disinhibited or 'relaxed' with the booze, and can't seem to function without it.

So how much, how regularly, and why you drink are good markers of problems. But there are others. Denial, secretiveness, solo drinking, and slowly increasing amounts all contribute. It may be that propensity to drinking is partly inherited. Thus it can be both nature and nurture, personal preference, and job stress.

We know that prohibition did not work. We know that restrictions often have serious drawbacks. Wise organizations model modest, occasional, after-work socialization drinking. Unwise organizations either ban it or send out contradictory signals.

Alcohol is a beneficial, legal, ancient beverage. There will always be alcoholics, but we can reduce their numbers.

Proactive people and sales performance

There are two types of people in the world: those who believe there are two types and those who do not. But it is easy and satisfying, even useful, to think in opposites and in types.

One distinction has been made in the sales field, which seems to make sense. It is the distinction between those people who are proactive and those who are reactive. Proactive people seek to change their environment. They tend to try to alter, exploit, and change in shape their interpersonal environment, their business world. They seek out situations that give them opportunities.

Proactive people also have other approaches to get on in their world. They cognitively restructure situations—that is, they tend to try to appraise, or construe, or perceive situations differently: they see problems as opportunities, and setbacks as learning experiences. And they evoke in others the reactions they want. They tend to be energetic, optimistic, 'go for it' types. Test yourself. Answer yes or no to the following questions.

1. I really enjoy (no really) challenges and obstacles to be overcome.
2. I know I am better than most at spotting business opportunities.
3. I am always into finding better, faster, cheaper, more efficient ways to do things.
4. I really like turning dreams into reality.
5. I am driven to make a difference.

6. I am happy to be called an opportunist. I look for opportunities.
7. I can and do champion unpopular but really creative ideas.
8. I don't let obvious obstacles prevent me from doing things.
9. I really enjoy challenging the routine.
10. I can turn around problems: see opportunities in setbacks.

Add up the number of 'yes' answers you gave. Seven or more and you sure are proactive.

So, what do we know about the proactive (as opposed to reactive) personality? These people tend to be sociable, hard working, and creative (extroverts, conscientious, open to experience). They have a strong need for achievement, for dominance. They tend to be active in extra-curricular and civic activities. And they tend to be elected leaders in groups.

Not surprisingly they tend to succeed in sales. One study of estate agents (published in the *Journal of Applied Psychology*, Vol. 80) found there were three important predictors of performance as measured by number of houses sold. Experience (years in the job) played a part. So did intelligence. Salesmen and women need to be bright enough. But the strongest predictor was the extent to which they had a proactive personality.

Not really a big surprise. People select, interpret, and alter their situations. They make their luck. But they do so best when they have some autonomy. Presumably part of the definition of the proactive person is that they seek out job situations that 'fit' their profile—that is, they are allowed to be proactive.

The proactive personality no doubt has as its motto 'carpe diem.' But such people don't just seize the day, they create it. They believe that you make your bed and you lie in it. You can and should create your opportunities as well as spot them.

The pensive, reactive, cautious person, happy to take a back seat, has no role in sales. The swashbuckling opportunist does best ... as long as they are bright enough, and able to plan and learn from their mistakes.

Psychogrammar

Perhaps it can be attributed to that quite unexpected runaway success, *Eats, Shoots, and Leaves*, which has already spawned spoofs such as *Eats, Shites, and Leaves*.

Perhaps it was all that free-thinking, self-expression-teaching philosophy of the 1960s that left a generation of educationally-challenged apostrophe users. The grammar-is-less-important-than-content school tried to persuade people that a knowledge of grammar was not necessary to produce good creative writing.

Perhaps it is due to txtng, or to computer programs that spell-check.

Perhaps it was reading e.e. cummings.

Whatever the cause, a renewed interest in, concern about, and fascination with correct grammar has seen a sudden rise in new psychiatric conditions hitherto unknown. These are psychogrammarian disorders that can render ordinary people hapless, helpless, and hopeless. Some are quite unable to put pen to paper, fingers to keyboard, or even read the documents of others.

But, once diagnosed, help is at hand. A mixture of discipline and practice can set one on the right road. So far, the following complaints have been recognized.

◈ *Adolescent exclamation mark compulsion*: a pre-morbid condition that often recedes in early adulthood, in which most sentences are ended with one or more exclamation marks!!! It indicates intensity of emotion for those with a limited vocab.

◈ *Incurable acronym dependency*: the inability to write any sentence without using some mysterious in-house acronym: 'The PMS Committee meets to discuss plans for STAGE 3 WOLOP implementation after BONGS.'

- *Undifferentiated apostrophe blindness*: a very common condition; sufferers have no idea where to put apostrophes or why. There are four possible variants: absence (never using them); random spreading (putting them anywhere at random); always wrong (never getting it right); and compulsive rewriting of sentences to minimize their use.

- *Chronic bullet-point impulse*: mainly found among scientists, PowerPoint presenters, and marketing people who cannot string sentences together into coherent stories. It may be accompanied by logo fixation.

- *Narcissistic capital letter condition*: often an indication of poor writing. The sufferer uses capital letters, sometimes for whole words, to shout. Commonly found in email correspondence.

- *Acute colon/semi-colon disorder*: characterized by the sudden over- and then under-use of colons; but more likely semi-colons. Writers believe, incorrectly, that these have more gravitas than mere commas.

- *Habitual commaphilia/phobia*: this may take the form of requiring a minimum of six commas per sentence to indicate curious, but necessary and desirable, pauses, or … paradoxically just never using them.

- *Hysterical hyphen hyperactivity*: this condition arises from an inability to recognize the appropriate place for commas, colons (and brackets), so hyphens—and dashes—are used.

- *Periodic italics obsession*: a primarily juvenile condition often found in those preferring to fiddle with pretty typeface options rather than getting on with the writing in the first place.

- *Episodic (parentheses) tendency*: sudden bursts of parenthesizing, even having to have subparentheses of different shapes ({ }). It has mysterious (and irrational) origins and consequences.

- *Pretentious vocabulary illusion*: usually a condition of the less educated. Sufferers always prefer to eschew obfuscation through the overuse of enigmatic, obscurantist, abstruse, and recondite phrases and metaphors.
- *Untreatable proofreading neurosis*: this can be either an obsessive-compulsive disorder, involving erasers, reading backwards, or saying things out loud for fear of letting through minor typos. On the other hand, it is characterized by cavalier narcissism, the whole activity being essentially trivial.
- *Crypto-dyslexic spelling disorder*: akin to apostrophe blindness, this is a cognitive spectrum disability which means that sufferers simply can't spell even the most simple words let alone get the classics like acomodation, seperate or definate right.
- *Residual typeface fetish*: a childlike desire to fiddle about with semi-illegible, quirky fonts. Often accompanied by green ink and black background disorder.

Rugged individualists

Sales jobs are on the increase. There may be as many as three to four million people in the UK with essentially sales or marketing jobs. And it's a difficult and often demanding job. The drop-out rate can be staggeringly high. Sales people are often difficult to manage because their job gives them high levels of autonomy.

Selecting the 'right' people is a serious business. To find that resilient, persuasive, energetic individual with impact, charm, and influence is problematic. But the pay-off can be particularly high. In fact, compared to most other jobs, the difference in output (and therefore profits) between the good and the bad, the average and the good, the good and the exceptional, is very large indeed. There may be few other jobs where getting the right workforce can contribute as much.

So, not unnaturally, quite some effort has gone into finding the characteristics associated with super sales staff. Everything has been looked at, from handwriting to intelligence. How important is skill, or aptitude, or personality? Can you pick them by depending entirely on their personal history (biography), some of which is found in a CV? How motivated or interested in the job itself do they have to be?

There has, in fact, been so much research in this area that reviewers have actually preferred meta-analyses. That is, they have gathered together all the (good) studies in the area and looked at the patterns in the results. From this they hoped to see what factors are important and use their predictive power when choosing sales people.

One such study was published in the prestigious American *Journal of Applied Psychology* (Vol. 83). The first thing to notice is that some studies used ratings (by managers, typically) as the criteria of success. Other used actual sales figures. And—surprise, surprise—they did not always give the same results.

Many personality traits were investigated. How extrovert, or stable, or likeable people were. Did the fact they were cooperative, or flexible, or dependable make a difference? And what of intelligence? Was being bright helpful? Did successful sales people have to have vocational interests that included selling? And what about their life story, age, education, number of dependants, work history, club membership?

The results showed three interesting facts. *First*, irrespective of whether the study had actual sales or ratings as the criteria, certain factors were consistently important. Good sales people were dependable, organized, persistent, and achievement-oriented. No substitute for hard work and conscientiousness. Next, they are, as one always notices, gregarious, sociable, outgoing, and assertive. They were also high-impact, energetic, influential people. There were other important predictors. Good sales people were able to use and had knowledge of established selling techniques. They also liked selling-type jobs.

Second, there were some factors that were related to supervisor ratings but not to sales revenue, and vice versa. Intelligence was a good example. It predicted ratings but not sales, as did age. So sales staff don't have to be bright, though managers might prefer them to be so.

Third, if you add some of these factors together, you can really improve your chances of getting the right person. Certainly being ambitious, hungry, and achievement-oriented counts for a great deal: more than education, experience, and intellect. And so does simple drive and being action-oriented. Psychologists call it potency.

Being emotionally stable, being able, having a good vocabulary, or a way with numbers, simply was not relevant.

There was even evidence that brighter people did less well. Being a rugged individualist did matter—decisive, action-oriented, and non-sentimentalist.

Yes, there are complications. It does depend to some extent on the following factors.

◆ The customer type: obviously products attract partic-ular customers. Age and stage, money and class, made a difference. And some sales people fit more easily their customers' profile.

◆ The product type: the product may be important. Perhaps bald men sell toupees better; perhaps beauty products for women are best sold by women; perhaps it takes a particular type of person to sell power tools.

◆ The economic cycle: selling is harder in a recession, but some products and processes seem immune to the slings and arrows of outrageous economic fortune.

Selection will never be a precise science. There are just too many confounding factors. But selecting the right person sure makes a difference in sales, as any one in the industry knows. So studies in this area are important both to confirm and challenge stereotypes and prejudices. They also let people know how powerfully various factors are predictive of sales success, so that they know where to invest their selection and training time and money.

Sales ethics

Have you got a CEO? That is, chief *ethical* officer, not chief executive officer? Have you or should you or will you pander to the populist cry for ethical self-examination? Can you make a good business case for paying attention to ethics? And what about sales organizations? Is the idea of a sales company actively, openly, and genuinely propagating ethical selling preposterously oxymoronic?

Does caveat emptor really mean be careful because sales people hide things, tell half-truths, and dissimulate? Can one make a case for sales ethics?

Certainly ethics is more and more 'on the table' in business. We have so-called ethical investments, fair-trade products, and ethnic group protection boycotts and actions.

If the customer is aware of ethics, the company must be too, and the sales staff. If customers have ethical questions you need to provide ethical answers. If they want ethical sales-staff behavior as a condition of purchase they get it. Then more so with frequent repeat purchase.

Manufacturing and sales teams like to be trusted. They know a reputation for integrity, honesty, and fulfilling their promises goes a long way. They know that a growing group of well-heeled customers now include ethics alongside cost and product features as buying criteria.

So are sales ethics customer driven? Do they consider sales ethics in the grand bazaar in Istanbul or in the farmers' market? Maybe not, but people return to stores they trust, that speak the truth, and that don't seem to be in the business of hoodwinking customers.

So all companies and even those in sales are beginning to ask quasi-ethical questions. Are ethics related to advertising *and* service? What is the payback from training and obeying a code?

There are, believe it or not, international codes of ethics for sales and marketing. Here are some examples of what they include.

◆ I pledge my efforts to assure that all marketing research, advertising, and presentation of product concepts are done clearly, truthfully, and in good taste so as not to mislead or offend customers.

◆ I shall not knowingly participate in actions, agreements, or marketing policies that prove detrimental to customers, competitors, or established community, social or economic policies and standards.

There are many of these wish lists. The Direct Selling Associations have the following three items.

◆ Abstain from encouraging you to purchase more inventory than you can sell in a reasonable amount of time.

◆ Repurchase, at not less than 90 percent of the original cost, any inventory and sales aids you have purchased within the past 12 months if you decide to leave the business.

◆ Explain the repurchase option in writing.

Yeah, yeah, yeah! Does your local second-hand car dealer do all this stuff? Certainly some sales organizations have better reputations than others.

Some sectors have been acutely aware of ethical issues. The pharmaceutical business is highly profitable. It involves persuading large numbers of doctors to prescribe one drug over another. Sometimes there are more reps than patients in the waiting room. And doctors are incentivized by meals and conferences in exotic destinations, by trinkets and toys, but also seriously expensive medical and non-medical gifts.

Doctors, like everyone else, differ in their ethical codes. Some will not even accept a sandwich or a pencil from any reps, or from reps from certain companies. Others draw a line on the value of the 'gift.' Some have interesting rationalizations and happily enjoy the largesse of all reps from all companies.

But voluntary codes are not enough. Doctors' practices and hospitals devise their own codes. And the law intervenes, too, though it may not use the word 'ethics.' Certain practices are pre- and proscribed, all aimed at ensuring that certain selling practices do not occur. The law is the last resort to protect the customer and ensure above-board practices.

Of course, customers do not want a pig in a poke. They all want a bargain, but some want more. They want to believe in the product, the manufacturer, and the selling organization. Purchasing products is increasingly politicized. Ethics can give you a competitive edge. But there is little worse than a company that trumpets ethics, which is then found to be all flim-flam, wrapping, and spin. Better not go down that track if you do not mean it.

Schadenfreude

Schadenfreude: the exquisite joy and smug satisfaction gained from contemplating and reveling in the misfortune of others. To see the mighty fallen.

It seems odd that we had to import this very German— and, for some, difficult to pronounce word. Why do we not have our own term for this concept?

Is Schadenfreude a particularly British obsession? A healthy attitude? It is said that the British, or at least the British tabloid press, really enjoy making, but then breaking heroes. There seems to be at least as much effort and joy in building someone up—be they guru, film star, sporting hero—as knocking them down to size. What goes up, apparently, must come down.

The Americans, however, admire the successful. They are held up as role models for others to aspire to. None of that European envy and sneering. But this jealousy of the successful has spread to the Antipodes. Did the British export it to their colonial cousins or did they happily import it from the Brits? Whatever, they do have their own slang for it: tall poppy pruning.

Actually the concept of the *tall poppy* can be found in the works of the Roman historian Livy, who noted how a fellow Roman decapitated the heads of the tallest poppies while walking in his garden. The message was conveyed to his son, who understood immediately the metaphor and got rid of all the chief men of state.

Schadenfreude, or tall poppy syndrome, is all about attitudes to high achievers. There are inevitably two extremes: those who admire and respect the successful and those who wish to bring them down a peg. So those in favor would agree:

- Successful individuals deserve all the rewards and recognition that they get.
- All societies need many very high achievers.
- It is important to encourage and support highly successful individuals.
- Most successful people are helpful and useful to others.

But those opposed to high flyers argue that:

- Very successful people soon get too big for their boots.
- Most successful people succeed only at the expense of others.
- Those successful high achievers who fall from grace almost always deserve to.
- It's really good to see very successful people fail occasionally.

Societies that exhibit Schadenfreude are often deeply ambiguous about any sort of achievement, and the status and prominence that comes with it. Thus high flyers are valued and praised for their efforts and ability, and the benefits they bring to wider society. But they must not exhibit hubris or complacency, or they will be punished.

At an individual level, more conventional, right-wing, authoritarian personalities favor rewarding the successful because the conventional generally submit to authority, accept socially sanctioned rules, and believe in showing respect.

How do people react when they see a successful figure fall? The answer, of course, lies in the extent to which you admire or agree with the person knocked off the pedestal. Most politicians know the experience: Clinton and Bush, Major and Thatcher, Mitterrand and Kohl, Hawke and Keating … all rose and fell.

Those who see their political enemies get their comeuppance experience sheer joy and glee, while their supporters can be quite disturbed by the experience. The former believe that the 'bad' tall poppy fully deserved it; there is a God, a just world. They savor the sweet taste of classic Schadenfreude.

Those who supported the culled, decapitated, and dismissed high flyer feel the shaky ground of what appears to be an unjust, unfair world populated by capricious, vicious, and retributive forces.

We have all experienced or witnessed Schadenfreude, but some actively seek it out. They could be seen as envious, vengeful, hostile individuals who waste their energy in attacking others rather than trying to achieve anything themselves. Envy is a social cancer that can eat into the soul. To be addicted to the emotion of Schadenfreude can be deeply destructive.

Scientist in residence

Prisons, universities, even big manufacturing companies sometimes have an 'artist,' 'poet,' or 'actor' in residence. Their mission may not be that clear, but poorly and very unevenly paid craftspeople may leap at the opportunity of a secure salary for a year. They probably also enjoy minor celebrity status, a blank canvas, and an opportunity to rub up against types they rarely come across.

The role of the craftsperson in residence is often seen to inspire. To inspire a love of work or literature or art. To teach how to express powerful and enduring emotions. Maybe even to heal. So just as we have art and drama therapy so our craftsperson in residence may still a troubled heart, or light a candle in the darkness of despair.

Some of these individuals have clearly done very good work in prisons, hospitals, and schools. They can help the poorly educated and inarticulate tell their story, find their voice, even confront their demons. Their effect on 'big strong boys' is often dramatic. And for the good they do, they might even be considered 'good value for money.'

But why stop at 'artist' in residence. Why not scientist, or statistician, or even psychiatrist in residence? The 'in residence' scheme should not be thought of as either charity or alternative to the dole. The aim is to give both individuals and parties a novel, rewarding, and enriching experience. Both gain, both educate, both enjoy.

So how would one use the scientist in residence? The stereotype of the impractical, emotionally volatile, unkempt artist may be no more accurate than that of the inarticulate, emotionally illiterate, over-technical scientist.

What are scientists good at? How could one use them?

Part depends on their science. Are they anatomists or chemists, physicists or mathematicians? But whatever their disciplinary training, they will presumably share assumptions and skills.

The first job of the scientist in residence is to inspire. Governments and universities in the West are very worried by the fact that young people are eschewing physics, chemistry, engineering, and math for media, sports, and gender studies. Yes, the sciences are 'hard,' and yes, they involve a lot of work, but most of all young people reject them because they are not 'sexy.'

Cooks rather than chemists, footballers rather than physicists, and actors rather than actuaries appear to fire the imagination. But most individuals can recall 'hard' science programs, lessons, and books that made a difference. Physics describes how the world works: it answers many practical everyday questions. And biology is the science of life. Can there by anything more fascinating?

There are probably three good reasons to have a scientist in residence. The first has been mentioned: it is to inspire. The second is to educate. Scientists ask different questions to business people. They are interested in causal mechanisms and processes. They are happy to entertain complexity and to try to work out how multiple factors and variables interact to produce outcomes. They build and test models and theories.

And scientists ask odd, difficult, sometimes rather peculiar questions. They like to challenge conventional wisdom, to probe orthodoxy, and to investigate the accepted ways of doing things.

Naturally, all this examination can be threatening and often annoying. But it is important, as we have seen in the evidence-based medical world, where many practices were seen as not only having no benefits but, worse still, doing actual harm.

But there is a third reason. And that is to sober up the scientist to the practical difficulties of everyday management. Scientists want ever greater amounts of money for their research. But many have little idea about money generation.

The theory and the practicality are often very different. Scientists seem flawed by public incomprehensibility and rejection of their theories. We have professors of the public understanding of science. Perhaps we need more of the scientific understanding of the public.

Scientists who have done a stint in business often return different people. Their sojourn or gap experience occasionally turns them into successful, even avaricious entrepreneurs.

The 'in residence' experience must be a two-way street. It must be mutually beneficial. It should not be seen as an amazing sinecure for those who can't find proper jobs. Nor should it be seen as beneficial to only one party.

The 'in residence' experience may serve as an excellent beneficially educational experience for both professional and organization. An excellent alternative to a sabbatical, or even an MBA.

MULTIPLE CONSULTANT DISORDER

It's easy to knock consultants. There are probably as many consultant jokes as there are lawyer jokes, and they are surprisingly similar. Such jibes are motivated by a potent mix of envy and contempt. Why should these people, who give so little, get so much? Why are they arrogant so-and-sos and cocky know-it-alls?

But perhaps we need to pity more than despise them. They seem to have short working lives. Burnt out, but opulent, they may have to start a second career in their early forties. And they are certainly at the mercy of market forces. Bull markets might mean Champagne and Porsches, but bear markets can easily mean retrenchment, retirement, and retraining. It's a rollercoaster ride for most of them.

And they do work long hours—often with dreary, difficult, or disaster-prone clients in firms that go under anyway. The business-class travel, the smart cars, and the expensive dinners don't make up for the fact that they spend most of the week completely exhausted. Cash rich, but time poor. Work–work imbalance. No quality time for anybody, really.

And the consultant jokes do get to them in the end. Many feel they don't deserve the bad press they get from constipated pen pushers in the public sector with secure pensions and a nice nine-to-five lifestyle. Many feel they deserve more respect, more praise and, some, even more money.

So they fret and moan. For some it is more serious. They develop a range of consultant-specific psychological problems. Many of these have just been recognized, but the list is growing. The following are among the more common.

- ◆ *Cathartic blue-sky regimen*: this consists of legitimately gazing out of the window, visiting exhibitions, even going fishing, while supposedly brilliant, novel ideas form and gestate in the back of the mind.
- ◆ *Bipolar budgetary reaction*: this is an obsession with the client's budget. How many consultants does it take to change a light bulb? The answer: 'How big is your

budget?' The swing is from concentrating on the work to how to sell more work to exhaust the budget.

◆ *Consistent cancellation charge neurosis*: some consultants love late cancellations because they get the money without having to do anything. The temptation is to make this a central pillar of the contract and to have very generous terms for themselves.

◆ *Post-traumatic contract fixation*: this involves both insisting clients sign outrageous contracts full of small print (what the big print giveth ...), and also a constant fiddling with documents in the belief that the client is trying to obtain extra work for no money.

◆ *Regenerative debriefing disturbance*: this consists of having a constant impulse to debrief everybody all the time about what is going on, the nature of the project's progress, and so on. However, it can manifest itself in the exact opposite way—that is, a phobia about any sort of debriefing update, such that nobody knows at any point what is going on.

◆ *Psychosexual empowerment compulsion*: the idea, now long discredited, that it is the job of consultants to empower staff to release their energy and enthusiasm. Experience should have taught them that this usually leads to angry, helpless managers and complacent, bewildered staff who have no idea what to do next.

◆ *Obsessional evaluative disturbance*: this is the paranoid belief that they are being evaluated by everybody all the time. It comes in two forms: feeling one is over-evaluated (assessed, checked up on, monitored) or that one is not being monitored enough to show what a brilliant and decisive job one is doing.

◆ *Adolescent facilitation malady*: this is the delusion that you need an overqualified, narcissistic, and garrulous consultant to facilitate every discussion and every meeting. It usually stems from a mixture of nosiness and paranoia.

◆ *Addictive feedback disorder*: this is the charming belief that everything is improved by feedback, or indeed that anyone knows what to do with it when they get it (like it or not). At extremely dysfunctional levels consultants spend their time doing little else other than asking for and giving feedback to random people in the organization by email, monitoring one-to-ones, or conducting quasi-appraisal exercises.

◆ *Habitual focus group syndrome*: this is the regression to an old favorite when stumped. It passes the time, is fully chargeable, looks like real work, gets sexy quotes, and can be justified.

◆ *Chronic gizmo fetish*: usually afflicting the middle-aged man deprived of Dinky toys and Meccano at a crucial point, this is the pathetic attempt to impress clients with state-of-the-art, wireless, super-minute technology that is pointless, expensive, and just says 'failed poser.'

◆ *Generalized gravitas delusion*: found in consultants of any age and stage, it is the need to have or, worse, to have recognized their personal intellectual gravitas, their wisdom, their heavyweight contribution. It is also known as delusions of grandeur or narcissist personality disorder.

◆ *Premorbid implementation tendency*: this is the near phobic desire to postpone the implementation phase of the project (as opposed to the planning phase), fearing it less fun, more effort and likely to show up the whole thinking as an airheaded, botched-up process.

◆ *Residual person substitute reaction*: this is the worry that clients will not realize or indeed object to the fact that the smart, wise, grey-templed consultant who sold the job will not deliver it. That will be done by a 24-yea- old stroppy MBA who's never done a proper day's work in his life.

◆ *Episodic professional impulse*: this happens during downtime or in depression, and involves getting a few old buddies to club together to found important-sounding quasi-professional bodies like academies, institutes and schools of advanced blah-di-blah. Makes sense ... very good for business

- *Undifferentiated revitalize dysfunction*: consultants like terms that suggest renewal, revival, and revitalization. They believe they can and do, like Lazarus, breathe life into the dead. They are, of course, profoundly wrong, misguided, and naive, but can come to believe in the myths.
- *Unconscious rightsize withdrawal*: we have been through downsize and capsize, yet still it is easy to increase profits by culling staff. This disorder is about not giving up a powerful impulse to randomly lay off crucial people in the name of short-term profit.
- *Organic systems tendency*: system building is often a trainspotting engineer's favorite activity. It is the belief that once you have some system, preferably electronic, in place all problems will automatically go away.
- *Atypical value-added disease*: this usually manifests itself in a neo-Buddhist repetitive mantra, such that all sentences are peppered with the V-A words. They become like a talisman, justifying all sorts of odd, and usually unnecessary, interventions.
- *Chronic work–life imbalance*: this results from the injunction to give all to the firm, to be fully committed, to be signed up for the great journey. Hey, this is the core of your life. Babies, families, and friends can wait!

Selling events

Over 100 years ago, Le Bon (a French sociologist) wrote a famous book on crowds. It was about the power of crowds to deindividualize and change people. In it he wrote: 'The miser becomes generous, the skeptic—a believer, the honest man—a criminal, the coward—a hero.' And he might have added 'the punter a purchaser and the inhibited shopper a frenzied bargain hunter.'

At another point he says, 'Among the other characteristics of crowds, we must note their infinite credulity and exaggerated sensibility, their short-sightedness and their incapacity to respond to the influences of reason. Affirmation, contagion, repetition, and prestige constitute almost the only means of persuading them. Reality and experience have no effect upon them.' A marketer's dream, then?

Le Bon is famous for his concept of deindividualization, which is the idea that people in crowds lose self-awareness. They laugh, cheer, and shout. And they lose their reason. Crowds engender a sort of madness.

Sales people have begun to understand and use the big event—the rock concert, football final, motivation speech, and political rally.

Big events can make attendees impressionable and impulsive, carefree and careless with their money. People may pay large sums of money for tickets to events. So what's a little extra money to buy a memento of a great occasion? There may be a post- or pre-show tented mall of stalls paying serious amounts for their turf. 'Ambush marketers' might target people in a post-event daze. Sports fans seem pretty caught up in a frenzy of commercialism: ads and logos appear on everything from tickets to turnstiles.

It has even been suggested that motivational seminars and courses provide an excellent opportunity to sell. Certainly the human potential gurus from the 1960s who encouraged all that subconscious exploration, primal screaming, and rebirthing have been replaced by a much more sophisticated lot. But they can be pretty confrontational.

So how to make a crowd receptive? Perhaps opening people up to new ideas is also an opportunity to sell them new products. A good start is rhythmic music and audience participation. Get them into a yes-response set with standard questions. 'Do you want to pay less tax?' Or 'Do you want more job security/a better work–life balance/fair appraisals?' Think of what happens at auctions.

There are 'proper' legitimate auctions such as those we see on the box more and more. But there are also those 'fly by night' street market guys who stir up a crowd, throw around a few free offers (as anglers scatter hook-free worms at a patch on the river) and have their well-appointed role-model, actor stooges.

Even the most sensible of people give themselves a limit when going to an auction (as they would at a race meet or casino). They know by personal experience and observation of others that it is easy to get carried away and pay both much more than you intended and, worse, more than the item is actually worth.

The charity auction exploits this crowd effect. You have had a good dinner and there are some interesting items for sale with a well-known celebrity as the auctioneer. He or she can tease, cajole, and even bully people into being more generous. People can and do pay ten times more than things are worth. But then that's part of the purpose of the chari-table event. The auction makes it more fun but also allows it to happen. And far from looking naive and gullible for paying over the odds, the bidders bask in their largesse, gaining in kudos what they have lost from their wallet.

But selling events can bring out the worst in people as well as the best. People will queue all night to be first into the store on the 'first day of *the* sale.' They may befriend each other in the cold, early hours, but once those doors are open it is every man for himself. Ugly, competitive, avaricious greed. No more, no less.

We are social animals. We imitate and conform. We all like to think of ourselves as level-headed, independently minded, sensible shoppers. Others may go mad in crowds and fall victim to group instincts. We like to believe that we are able to keep our head, while all around are losing theirs. But, alas, the data suggest otherwise …

Selling to oldies

Don't underestimate the grey market. Never in history have people lived so long and had so much money. The baby boomers are taking retirement. And many are loaded. So companies are wondering how to target them.

Of course, there are products that appear to be aimed solely at the not-so-young. Stairlifts, walk-in baths, and comfy slippers; safe and affordable vacations; insurance plans. But many of the early campaigns backfired because they stereotyped older people.

The more common stereotypes are that old people are socially isolated from family and society as a whole; in poor shape mentally and physically; quite unable to learn new things; bored and boring; and certainly not interested in rumpy-pumpy.

One question is when people can be officially classified as old or elderly. The answer seems to be about 10 to 20 years older than you are now. So to 20 year olds, 40 year olds appear to be well past their sell-by date, while 70 year olds who cheerfully talk about 'old people' never include themselves in the equation.

Sales people and organizations often try to understand their potential market with some sort of segmentation. This can utilize financial or geographic variables, but more often include activities, interests, and opinions. This is called psychographics and tries to sum up the lifestyle of older people. This, in theory, helps determine how they are targeted and personally sold to.

Psychographic researchers often come up with catchy titles for key groups of consumers, such as Personal and Persuadable, Defensive and Disengaged, Self-sufficient and

Satisfied. But with the help of gerontologists, psychologists, and sociologists they have developed fairly robust and reliable groupings.

Some older people seem well adjusted overall. Some readjust and reorganize their lives according to their new circumstances. They celebrate rather than mourn, and actively enjoy new experiences. They find new activities, new friends, a new persona. Others drop many activities but focus on those that gave them pleasure in the past.

Another group, though well and well-off, are not so well adjusted. They may be in denial about their age and their retirement, and may have a deep fear of being stereotyped. They were probably achievement oriented and hard working, and would like to keep it that way. Some welcome the label and status of retirees seeking support and succor away from the rollercoaster, stressful world of work. Some become obsessed with their physical well-being, seeing it as their best hope for being happy.

And, of course, there are groups that really don't cope well at all. They can be angry, apathetic, or depressive. Angry people can be paranoid or celebrate their victimhood. They often look back on their life, seeing only disappointment, failure, and missed opportunities. The apathetic take happily to their rocking chairs, feeling unable to change their life circumstances. The depressed have given up, and see themselves as failures in the lottery of life. What the astute sales person wants to know is essentially three things: the adjustment level and lifestyle of the older person, their financial situation, and their hot buttons.

Advertisers have learnt to portray old people as dynamic and vigorous, not old and decrepit. They may be lined and grey but they are handsome, fit, and energetic. Those who endorse products use the right words and visuals to portray this image. Older people are shown as part of the mainstream—not isolated, ghettoized, or gated. They are often shown with their families and making inter-generational decisions.

And the message? We all like quality and value, but concepts that resonate with the older consumer include comfort, dependability, and security. Perhaps most of all the ideas of independence, control, and self-efficacy resonate best. Old people like to know that the new product will enable them to be in control of their lives.

And the message must focus on the solution not the problem, and on the experience not the product. So the message for the shopping scooter is not the difficulty in getting to the supermarket, or the shiny new model, but how you can happily get about, do your shopping, visit friends in comfort and style.

So understand your market; speak to the audience clearly (not loudly) in upbeat positive tones; use familiar language … and don't mention the Golden Girls.

Sentence completion

My biggest regret in life is … Compared to most others of my age and stage I am considerably more … The thing I fear most is … Secretly I really admire …

These are called sentence-completion techniques. They are used by lazy and uninspired journalists to fill newspaper and magazine columns. They are interview techniques without the interviewer. And they offer the responder a wonderful opportunity to show off, to disclose, or to carefully manage others' impressions.

Many people loath open-ended questions on forms. Why do you want to work for this company? Explain how your particular experience and abilities make you an ideal person for this job? The amount of space available to answer these questions is positively correlated with both anxiety and frustration on the part of the respondent. A few rejoice at this opportunity for what psychologists call impression management. An opportunity to put one's best foot forward. To give the selector what she/she wants to hear. To express in your own words your own unique, fascinating, and very desirable aptitudes, abilities and skills.

But some people, indeed a fair percentage, stop at the open-ended questions and fail, therefore, to apply. They seem at a loss as to how to answer those questions in writing that they may well be asked face to face.

This fact has been known to selectors for some time. One easy and cheap way to separate the wheat from the chaff is to make the applicant do some work. Write a short essay (2000 words) is a simple serious selection criterion. The lazy, the 'not-sure,' and the bluffers stop there. It's all too difficult compared to answering simple questions.

But who uses sentence-completion techniques in business, and why? The answer is clever consultants, among others.

The rationale behind sentence completion is three-fold. *First*, and perhaps most important, to get at motives and motivation. The problem with many motivations—motives for power and dominance, motives for inclusion and affiliation, motives for achievement and success—is not that people *will not*, but that they *cannot* tell you.

Could famous politicians, entrepreneurs, or scientists tell you what drives and motivates them? They could, no doubt, give you an answer. But it might be a politically correct or self-justifying story, not actually the truth.

And this is the *second* reason for using projective techniques. They are, it is argued, much less prone to faking, dissimilation, or social desirability. People 'see through' questionnaires, but much less so sentence completion. The scorer looks for the themes that they contain and is prepared to entertain contradiction and paradox.

Faking comes in two types: impression management and self-delusion. The former means giving answers to try to create a particular impression, such as being clever, charming, socially empathic and the like. It is the art of actors. Self-deception or delusion, on the other hand, is reporting in good faith something that is not actually true. Some people think they have a keen sense of humor when you know they clearly do not. Some believe quite genuinely that they are unattractive when they very definitely are, or, much worse, the other way around.

The *third* reason why people like and use sentence-completion tests is the mystery that surrounds them. Lay people love the Freudian unconscious stuff. They like to think of themselves as complex individuals with lots of hidden potential. Personality tests reduce an individual to as few as five or six numbers. It seems to many that you answer the test by saying how you typically behave and then the testers, using slightly different language, tell you back how you behave.

But projective techniques have an air of mystery. They can, it is argued, bring up long-forgotten memories and provide a genuine and unusual self-insight. The test brings things into awareness. It acts as a tool of discovery.

Academics are not keen on these tests. They claim they are unreliable in two senses, and that which is unreliable cannot be valid. First, people seem to give very different answers on different occasions. Their mood seems to influence how they respond. Second, two 'testers,' or examiners, appear to read quite different things into the same responses.

So. A party game? The manifestation of lazy journalists? Or a perspicacious method of plumbing the psyche? Discuss.

Service with a snarl

We are now a service rather than a manufacturing economy. Everything, it seems, is made in China. As a consequence, many young people find themselves in service jobs, be it on the telephone or face to face.

The British, it is said, have problems with service. They confuse it with servile. The Americans don't, or at least didn't, seem to have that problem. But things might be changing. The Brits are learning how to be quietly assertive. They are beginning to take service seriously and businesses are having to respond. They are encouraged in hotels and airplanes to complete customer feedback forms, which are often mainly about service.

And organizations are becoming very aware of selecting and training the right people. They want self-confident, sociable, socially skilled people who like teamwork and who can follow procedures. They need to be alert, switched on, and observant. They need to be organized and to set themselves high standards of cleanliness, neatness, and tidiness. They need to be diligent and honest.

Good service people need a good memory. They need to be emotionally stable and resilient: thick skinned, and not too upset by criticism. They certainly need energy. And they need to be results oriented. A tall order for poorly paid, poorly educated people, often working in a second language.

Equally important is to devise a short, robust, comprehensive test to measure customer perceptions of service quality. An interesting question is what dimension of customer service to evaluate. One well-known measure, SERVQUAL, originally published in the *Journal of Retailing*, suggests that five factors are important. The *first* is to do with the tangible side of things—the rooms, seats, tables, and staff. Are they modern-looking, aesthetically appealing, neat and clean? Do they all work properly? Have they been well designed?

Second, there are issues about the reliability of the service. Does the service provider get the order/booking/arrangement right first time? Do they fulfill their verbal and written promises? Are they consistent from place to place, time to time, individual to individual? Yet with all the reliable standardization, can they keep the touch personal?

Third, there are issues around responsiveness. Naturally, this refers to how promptly service people respond to requests. But it also refers to their attitude. Do they seem too busy? Too distracted? Are they doing it grudgingly? Do they fulfill the expectations they have set for themselves?

Fourth, and perhaps most interesting, is the dimension of assurance. Do the service people instill in you a sense of confidence that they know what they are doing and why? Do they seem to have the knowledge to answer your questions? Are you assured they are competent at the job?

Finally, there is empathy. Do you believe they have your best interests at heart? Do they try to understand your specific needs? Do they give you individual attention and try to see the world from your perspective?

Service is not about cost, though of course the two are related. It's about how organizations deliver. And it is becoming more and more significant in the growing homogenized service industries. It is, for many, the point of differentiation for the customer. And that must really be important.

Seven selling secrets

There are far fewer books on how to sell than how to manage. But much of management is about selling: selling ideas, concepts, and lifestyle choices. Selling is about persuasion, about attitude change, but most of all about behavior change.

There are huge industries dedicated entirely to the dark art of persuasion. The advertising industry, the PR industry, many public bodies, even charities, are there simply to persuade people to behave differently.

So what does it take to be a successful persuader? Is it some exceptional talent that is required, or is it a series of skills and processes? Certainly exceptional sales people appear to share particular characteristics. They tend to be socially skilled and optimistic. They don't blame the customer, the product or themselves for lack of closure ... they move on. They tend to be charming, socially aware, and friendly. Perhaps they have higher than average EQ. And they tend not to believe in luck: they propagate their own luck. Many are energetic, ambitious go-getters.

Surprisingly, introverts can make good sales people, though they have to *behave* more like an extrovert. They clearly do need to be tenacious in hard times. Most of all they need to know some of the central skills. Or are they tricks or principles? People who have studied the issue know that some persuasive or selling techniques work better than others.

❖ *Attraction*: people believe, like, and buy from those who apparently like them. Sales people befriend quickly; they use your first name a lot; they look for things they have in common with you. Some arrange home parties

(Tupperware and such like). Good sales people admire and praise your taste; ask about your likes. They try to short-circuit friendship formation.

- *Authority*: most people defer to education, expertise, and professionals. To have authorities, celebrities, and even newsreaders or failing actors endorse products or policies helps. Nine out of ten dog owners, four out of five dentists recommend … are attempts to exploit this principle. So establish your credentials and you enhance your credibility.

- *Consistency*: we in the West seem afraid of being inconsistent, of going back on our word, of contradicting ourselves. So the clever sales person gets people to say things: 'I need a new …,' 'I would buy if the price were right,' 'I am most eager to ensure my family is safe.' Then, having got this assurance, the sales person exploits it by showing how buying the product follows logically from what was said. Fear of being thought a liar, a hypocrite, or simply inconsistent makes the 'trapped' individual feel obliged to buy.

- *Reciprocity*: we have a strong culturally based urge to repay favors. Buy someone a drink and they reciprocate. Send a Christmas card and you receive one in return. Get given a thimble of wine at a trade show and you are more likely to buy. Get a 9-cent pen in a charity letter and donations go up. People return the favor in kind even when it is both unsolicited and unwanted. Arrive at a house with a cake and a plant to the value of less than $20 and your chances of selling a product worth $4000 are doubled.

- *Scarcity*: people want both to be like others but also superior to them. They love the idea of exclusivity. Hence all the blurb about 'limited edition' or 'last one left.' How many times have we heard 'last few days of sale' or 'while stocks last.' Some sales people claim to have secret information about things running out or becoming available. It could cause stampedes in old centrally run socialist economies.

◈ *Sexy*: people like to have their taste flattered. They all like to think they are kind, wise, and compassionate. And they like to think they have impeccable taste. People want to be at the cutting edge of style, new thinking, and consumption. The more they are told this the more they buy.

◈ *Peer pressure and proof*: we are sensitive to the beliefs and behaviors of our peers—people such as our work colleagues, neighbors, and friends, whom we like and trust. Told that most of them have bought a product, signed a petition, or made a donation, we are all much more likely to follow suit.

Sales people are taught these techniques. They often have to master complicated scripts that weave these concepts in and out at various stages. The sales person arrives with a gift (reciprocity), points out he knows the area because six neighbors have bought the product (peer proof), and really admires your living room design (attraction). Then he tries to get you to say certain things, which he will pick up later (consistency). He may establish his credibility, or that of a designer, inventor, or recent purchaser, to increase his authority and will have lots of material to 'sex up' the product.

Sound familiar? Of course ... there is nothing really new in sales except the increasing sophistication of all bodies, particularly charities and political parties, in exploiting them.

Sex at work

Perhaps the oddest thing about sex is that we can now all talk about it a great deal but still 'do it' under very restricted circumstances. Serious newspapers have therapists telling it to us straight. Toddlers have rudimentary 'birds and bees' talks before they can count. But sex at work—talk or action—is a serious no-no. We can talk about, and are encouraged to accept, numerous variants of sexual preferences but sex remains something you can't discuss or practice in the office. It is difficult for all sorts of reasons. Married couples at work are prone to nepotism. Having an affair leads to accusations of favoritism, immorality, or power-play. And the act of rumpy-pumpy in the office is really very unacceptable ... even at the Christmas party.

Taboo, prohibition, and secrecy are the agents of ignorance. How can we be an empathic, compassionate, and informed society without openness? Are there sex-related psychiatric disorders that go unnoticed and untreated? Are we really no better than the Victorians? We need to understand sexual pathology in the workplace. Could sexologists help out? The following is a 'first draft' of possible problems stalking the modern office.

- *Anticipatory appraisal aversion*: this is the deep, almost visceral, loathing and phobia associated with having to conduct appraisals on diffident, difficult, or doomed staff. Total aversion is the major cause of performance management virginity.
- *Board member frotteurism*: this is similar to *ostentatious osmotic dependency*. It is the delusional belief that (literally) 'rubbing up against' powerful board members

gives one special powers, privileges, and promotional opportunities.

- *Bonus fantasy paraphilia*: the patient experiences intensely arousing visions of obscenely large bonus payments occurring after a strictly average year.

- *Chronic premature articulation*: this is the constant urge to speak before (a) knowing what one wants to say, (b) being asked to speak, and (c) considering the consequences of career-limiting, egocentric business babble.

- *Competitor strategy voyeurism*: an uncontrollable obsession with what others are doing in the marketplace. It can lead to *eye-off-the-ball myopia*.

- *Dysfunctional conference exhibitionism*: this is linked to *adolescent show-off impulse,* involving self-obsessed narcissistic displays of emotion and heroic personal stories at all conferences.

- *Health and safety sado-masochism*: this is the unrelenting and unforgiving urge to inflict pain on oneself and others, possibly alternating, by being difficult-to-impossible about locked doors, temperature gauges, and access.

- *Hypo- or hyperactive sixual desire*: the latter is the more common complaint and revolves around the obscenely early (in terms of years) desire and demand to be paid a six-figure salary. Hypo-active desire occurs after years of failure and a preference to waste energy sniping at others who succeed.

- *New logo obsession*: a corporate police issue where every document, PowerPoint presentation, and internal memo must contain the new (very expensive) logo in the right colors, at the right angle, and in the right place.

- *Office supplier fetishism*: this may be manifest in curious ways—spending hours poring over stationery catalogues, sniffing certain products, prohibiting the use of some and prescribing the compulsory use of other items on irrational grounds.

◆ *Open-plan screen erectile dysfunction*: the inability to erect tall enough screens in an open-plan office to create the altogether natural and satisfying feeling that one is closed-plan again. This may be caused by strict nannies with rules about big erections in the office.

◆ *Premature promotion syndrome*: this is characterized as a youthful disorder where young people are not prepared to 'do their time' among the troops, wanting senior manager status long before their time.

◆ *Vice president identity disorder*: this is caused by working for one of those mid-Atlantic organizations where everybody is an executive vice president. It results in not really knowing if one is important or not.

◆ *Virtual team vaginismus*: this is a fear and phobia of the V-word—knowing that virtual is virtually nothing. It can result from trying bizarre email or phone brain-storming groups with bleary-eyed New Zealanders or bewildered Japanese at odd times of the day.

◆ *Wash-room gossip arousal*: this is akin to *luvvy-lavvy excitement* and results from the realization that the best grapevine is found in the office toilets where literally pissed-off managers pour out their venom about the grown-ups.

◆ *Work–life balance aversion*: this is caused by the shocking realization that one is better off staying at work, with all the power and structure processes in place, than going home where chaos rules.

Shop 'til you drop

They call it 'consumer behavior' at business schools, but we call it shopping. Should we have 'professors of shopping science' to help us understand the psychological processes involved in this common (almost daily) activity? Could there be a science of shopping to help stores maximize their profits?

Certainly, many myths surround the topic. Take the top three conspiracy theories about supermarket layout.

1. *The two staples—bread and milk—are furthest apart to keep you walking the aisles and then, en route, inevitably impulse buying.* No, they are in different places mainly for temperature reasons.
2. *Supermarkets deliberately try to disorient you by moving the stuff around.* No they don't, because relocating goods really annoys punters and sales drop if they do this regularly. Sure, changes are made, but the aim is to accommodate new stock or eliminate poor-selling ranges.
3. *They pile up big fruit and veg at the front of the store to encourage you to take a trolley, which you feel compelled to fill.* No, shopping trolley decisions are made before you enter the store.

But there are people watching and measuring behavior in all stores to try to understand consumer behavior. There are three methods of collecting shopping science data. First, a careful examination of stock, cash, and sales. That's quite simple and reliable. Loyalty cards make it easier. These can provide good data on consistency of time and exact details of your purchases. Associations can also be examined—for example, those who buy pesto are more likely to buy balsamic vinegar; those who buy own-brand also buy BOGOFs.

This data tells us about behavior, but it can't inform us about motives, which we have to infer. Or, if we believe people both will (and can) tell us about their real (conscious and unconscious) motives, we could interview them. Or they can be stopped before they enter and after they leave stores (noting differences between shopping intentions and actual purchases), or in ubiquitous focus groups, or even on the phone.

And then we can watch people shop. Through security cameras or using anthropologically trained observers, you can describe how people move through stores: what seems to slow them down or attract them to particular areas while shunning others, and why they appear to inspect physically some items and not others.

Retailers are interested in particular questions: the conversion rate (the number of people entering stores who actually purchase anything); the interception rate (the number of customers who interact with staff members); how long people actually spend in a store and how long they have to wait for service, especially to pay.

Time spent in a store is the single best predictor of how much is spent, so slowing people down is a good thing. But it is not a good idea to slow them down with poor signage and blocked aisles. Mirrors slow people down; intriguing displays do likewise. Equally, having to wait is the single best predictor of dissatisfaction, so it pays to ensure waiting is kept to a minimum.

Studies show many pretty obvious things. Signage is very important; people like to sit down in stores; music and smells can affect moods and thence purchases. People need ways of carrying things easily, and they tend to have habitual ways of moving around a store.

But what about individual differences? Yes, there are, of

course, shopper types: experiential and adventure shoppers; shopaholics and shopaphobics; economic shoppers and price-insensitive Johnnies; bargain hunters and sociable shoppers.

And are there demographic differences? Naturally shoppers have been classified by age, sex, and class. And this is where the fanciful speculation starts. Observers notice, people self-report, and loyalty card information indicates sex differences.

Females spend more time shopping than men. They seem to be more aware, inquisitive, and patient in stores. Men, it seems, move faster, look less, and are less inclined to ask questions. Men seem to worry less about price and seem more anxious to get out of the store.

Men inhibit women shoppers. Women accompanied by men spend half the time than if accompanied by other women. Women advise, consult, talk, suggest to each other … men get on with it.

Women, some socio-biologically inclined researchers note, find shopping relaxing and rejuvenating. But men are hunter-gatherers. They need a clear objective (i.e. a list) and to know precisely what brand, color, size, and style, where to go, how long to stay, and so on. Men go for the quick kill.

And then there are the pathologies associated with shopping addictions and compulsions, including shoplifting. There seem to be a disproportionate number of women suffering from these. People shop to confirm their identity (you are what you wear), to find external symbols of missing internal needs, or to restore a feeling of group belonging. Addictive shoppers are like anorexics—they feel empty inside, they need control and to feel admired.

The thesis is developed further with the concept of retail therapy. The shopper really is a profoundly unhappy person trying to 'buy relief' in big stores.

So it seems we may need professors of shopping science to explain to us why we feel, act, and think so oddly in stores.

Stress and strain

There have been two relatively recent changes in how people understand stress at work. The first is that it is endemic: everybody, everywhere, in all jobs, seems to have a lot of it. The second is that stress comes from the outside: it is caused to one. Long hours, nasty bosses, and government-imposed targets are seen to be major factors in stress.

Certainly, any historical perspective on work makes both claims pretty dodgy. The conditions under which our grand-parents worked were unquestioningly much more stressful than today, on all criteria. Furthermore they believed, rightly, that stress comes from both the outside and the inside. That is, there are and were stress-prone individuals. There were (perhaps are) even over-the-counter-medicines like Sanatogen Nerve Tonic and Quiet Life tablets.

Nerves-nervous-neurotic-negative affectivity. Neuroticism was recognized by the Ancient Greeks (specifically Galen) and is recognized by all modern-day psychologists. Neuroticism is also known as trait anxiety, but is now more usually called by its politically correct name: 'negative affectivity'. So what is it? Essentially, it is defined as a mood-dispositional dimension (people are consistently moody, stable, up and down), reflecting a pervasive, individual difference (it's consistent and enduring over time) in the experience of negative emotion and poor self-concept. People thus afflicted are gloomy, anxious, depressed, phobic, and feel bad about themselves.

Nearly all neurotics know they are. It, like all traits, is normally distributed in the population. Many people are calm, stable, and hardy. Some jobs demand it: airplane pilot, bomb disposal personnel, surgeon. But many are very unstable.

What researchers have discovered of late will not surprise many. If you carry out stress surveys in any profession or organization you get surprisingly high reports of stress. Even the most secure, unpressured, and controllable of jobs appears to give its incumbents stress. But if you measure the personality of individuals at the same time, what is apparent is that neurotics are reporting very high levels of stress and stable individuals low stress.

In other words, stress also comes from the inside. It is about how people perceive and react to their circumstances. Some see threat, insult, and innuendo where others see joviality. Some see a rude, ruthless, and over-demanding boss where others see someone under pressure, struggling to meet targets. Some perceive health hazards, personal prejudice, and ubiquitous unfairness where others see a happily functioning work environment.

This is not to deny that some work environments are psychologically toxic and massively stress inducing. The question, however, is to do with the role of trait neuroticism in the whole issue. It's very important from many points of view: from the legal perspective on creeping work stress and the likelihood of litigation; from the management perspective on absenteeism, morale, and productivity; from the selection perspective on finding happy, healthy employees.

But what is the role of neuroticism in stress at work? What is the process? There are essentially four possibilities. *First*, neurotics report, perceive, and experience more work stress and strain irrespective of the actual work conditions. Stress here lies in the eye of the beholder.

Second, neuroticism is a moderator; meaning that an individual's level of neuroticism determines how they respond to actual work pressures. In other words, neurotics do not have very good coping strategies. They seem super-sensitive to threats of all sorts, and their reactions to the normal daily hassles of work overpower them and lead to reports of high stress.

Third, neuroticism is a mediator variable, meaning that neurotics suffer stress because of the way they view their work environment. Their particular lens leads them to be over-sensitive to issues others do not react to. Their hyper-vigilance, sensitivity, and low(ish) self-esteem leads them to experience work as stressful.

The *final* possibility is that of neuroticism as a confound. In short, work conditions have little to do with stress: the association is spurious and illusory. Neurotics see all work environments as stressful; they experience more stress and strain. And that's it.

Naturally, psychologists have been eager to test out these various models. Not only because that is the 'business' of academic psychologists, but also because it has such important implications for interventions.

So what's the answer? Not so simple, alas. There is evidence for all four possible causal explanations. But it depends a lot on how one measures stress and strain. It could be measured by psychological symptomatology, or absenteeism, or medical reports of anxiety or depression. It could be measured by overall job satisfaction or dissatisfaction.

We do know three things. First, neuroticism is implicated strongly in all reports of stress at work. Second, neurotics do see more threats and challenges than non-neurotics, and cope with them less well. Third, other factors inevitably play a part, especially emotional support from co-workers and on-work sources.

Of course this has implications for selection, management, and training. And it does mean that we have to think more clearly about what surveys about stress at work mean and what we should do about them.

Super sales staff

Turnover in all sales jobs is remarkable. It is well over 90 percent per annum for many insurance companies. Whether selling cars or computers, insurance or insulation, furniture or double glazing, it is a hard job. It's not the low-base-rate, high-commission package; it's not the capriciousness of customers; it's not even the price. It's a tough, remorseless job that needs people with special characteristics.

Consult any company's sales people figures and you are bound to find the following: a few—possibly very few—superstars. These people double their difficult targets. And they seem to do so year after year. There are a large number of sales people who never approach their target and either they themselves or their company decide it's really not the job for them.

So what does it take? What are the characteristics of these super sales people? It's not intelligence or education. It's not always having a particular personality profile. There are six crucial factors that go to make up the successful sales person.

1. *Resilience, ego strength, optimism*: selling is about coping with rejection. Call ten people, three are prepared to listen and one to buy. Most people say no (no thank you) every day. So 90 percent of the time one is faced with rejection. Easy to search for blame: the product, the price, the management, the economy. Easy to get depressed and less active, which leads, of course, to a vicious circle of despair. The super sales person needs to be robust, resilient, and to believe in themselves. They need an optimistic outlook, frame of mind, and take on the world. Setbacks need to be dealt with

swiftly. Learn and move on. Strong self-belief in making your own luck is a core and crucial requirement. It's probably number one.

2. *Social skills, emotional intelligence, charm*: call it what you will, it's that easy-going approachableness. Sales people need to be perceptive. They are often trained to read the signals—body language and the like. And they also need to be very self-aware and to know how others see them. They also need the ability to change their own and others' emotional state. They cannot afford to let personal setbacks influence how they deal with new customers. They need to know how to regulate their mood state. And they need to know how to persuade others. Many of the tricks of the trade can also be taught. But one needs to be naturally good at this. Sales people need to be people watchers, street smart, and likeable.

3. *Hunger, ego drive, need to achieve*: being driven by loadsa-money, the fast car, and the usual paraphernalia of success is not enough. The really good ones get their kicks not from the results of the sale but from closing the deal. They know about hunt, bring down, kill. They understand 'getting to yes.' The really good ones take selling as a challenge, a source of pride, and as a mission. The intrinsic thrill of the job is in steering people to the orgasmic end point. It's part of their self-definition. Start selling just for the commission and you soon become extrinsically motivated. And you know what? It shows.

4. *Conscientiousness, orderliness, planning ability*: sales people usually hate paperwork. Pity, because it's pretty crucial to the whole endeavor. The financial people need the figures; someone has to invoice; the cash flow is important. The books need keeping. Just as important is planning strategies, mapping regions. This is not

something that can be done in the car with a mobile phone. This is a quiet, office-based activity. It takes discipline, dutifulness, and deliberation.

5. *Energy, enthusiasm, activity*: sales people need to be mentally and physically fit. The job is often physically demanding, involving long hours of travel, meetings, and the like. It's also emotionally demanding having to be attentive to people the whole time. Sales people are active—most are stimulus-seeking extroverts on the lookout for variety—but they need to know how to use, spend, and conserve their energy. It's a bit like eating bananas and oatmeal rather than chocolate. Energy is attractive: a sign of youth, a sign of commitment. It's not easy to fake over any period of time.

6. *Opportunism, spotting gaps, trend awareness*: the British despise opportunists who, they believe, somehow do not deserve what they get. But opportunists not only make opportunities, they look out for them. Such people spot a gap in the market; they notice that a competitor is having difficulty; they know if a product line is faulty. They act quickly and exploit the opportunity. But opportunity is not luck. All successful sales people know that you make your own luck. They also know that things happen fast in the business world. They know that flexible and adaptable is good. And that means looking out for these things.

A tall order? Resilient, charming, hungry, conscientious, fit, opportunists? Sure. These characteristics don't quite 'go together' much in nature. That is why people who have them are rare. Find and nurture them. Give them direction and support and you've got it made.

The advertising surround

Have you noticed how, on commercial television, cooking programs are interspersed with (or interrupted by) cooking ads, and car programs with ads for motor cars and related products? An eminently sensible strategy? Perhaps not.

Having ads congruent with programs seems, on the face of it, a no-brainer. People watch the program because they are interested in the products and processes so you have a nicely preselected and receptive audience for your wares. Would it not be daft to try to sell a car in a cooking program? Or have a funny ad in a tense melodrama?

Newspaper, radio, and television advertisements appear in a context. So do billboards, for that matter. The question is how the context affects the reception of the advertisement. Is congruent better than incongruent? Does one have a better chance of brand recognition or memory if there is congruency?

In academic jargon the issue is known as advertisement–product congruity. Researchers have noted that the general mood created by the surrounding environment can affect reaction to, and memory of, the advertisement. Some believe people react to all ads better when they appear in a happy program, but others think you need a good congruous fit: if you have an unhappy ad (say, for a charity or a medicine) then best place it in a sad program.

Construct accessibility theory believes congruity is best. Place a DIY product ad in a DIY program because the program will prime or stimulate the memory about similar issues. You activate a memory trace or pathway. So think about the program or those similar to it and you remember the ad. Also the program context may predispose viewers to pay more attention to the ads.

On the other hand, cognitive interference theory believes that a sort of information meltdown occurs, so that the program and ad merge together, resulting in impaired recall. Interestingly there seems to be more evidence for this side: *incongruity* is memorable.

But there are other factors in all this. One is audience involvement. We have all had the experience of being totally absorbed by a particular program, possibly with suspense or excitement, only to have the crucial moment spoilt by an ill-timed ad break. Annoyance at program interruption represses memory. Also, viewers watching a highly involving program will find it more difficult to pay sufficient attention to the ads. Their acute emotional experiences are cognitively demanding and very absorbing, thereby hindering the taking-in of new information (i.e. details in the ad) not directly related to the emotional experience.

Others, of course, argue that as the level of viewer involvement increases so does recall for ads. Again, the evidence is equivocal but most supports the high-involve-ment, low-recall theory.

Of course, many other factors affect advertisement recall. The age, education, and social class of the viewer. The time of day. The motive for and choice of television channels.

So you want people to pay attention to and recall your brand? Best choose to place it in a program not closely related to your product and not that absorbing.

PRO-TIREMENT

To retire is to withdraw, retreat, recede. You can retire from work
and retire from the world to become a recluse. You can retire into
yourself, becoming uncommunicative and unsociable. You can
retire well, both at football and from a job. But you can retire
hurt, retire angry, retire unwillingly and unhappily.

In the old days people retired to live their last few years,
often in poor health, before they died. The image was of the
individual with declining power, prestige, and influence.
Sucked dry, spat out, of little use to family or society as a whole.

Now it has a positive image. But there are caveats. Happy
early retirement requires various things.

- Good physical and mental health.
- Adequate finance, which is, indeed, a moving target.
- A vibrant and largish social support network.
- A structured, intrinsically motivating activity.

It is the last point that is perhaps the most interesting and
paradoxical. Happily retired people need a sort-of job or
occupation. They need something to give them a sense of
purpose, in cooperation with other people, that they find
interesting and valuable.

But now people retire earlier and live longer. They might
have 30 years of life after retirement. So things have been
changing. *First*, because the one-job-for-life era appears to
have passed, people now retire more than once. They may
retire many times, becoming serial retirees. There may be
retirement villages, but there are also retiring occupations.

Second, employers rather like these young-old retirees. It
used to be believed that you should never trust anyone over
30 years of age. Now it is the opposite. The older employee is
seen as more conscientious, more socially skilled, more
trusted, and more trustworthy.

Third, the clear distinction between working and retirement is now increasingly blurred. There are volunteers who
do unpaid work with all the appearance (and benefits) of
work, but no salary. There is a wide variety of part-time jobs,

from the well-heeled non-executive director to the store clerk who works mornings only.

Retired people may be called back in time of crisis to be an interim manager, a position they really enjoy. They feel valued, important, pleased to help out. Certainly, professionals who retire are often very different from the less skilled. They like to keep their identity and title. Hence Emeritus Professor or Captain Smith RN (Retired). And their years of education make them adaptable and eager to learn.

Many volunteer organizations are heavily staffed by retired people who were brought up with the pro bono publico mottoes. Both groups benefit from the experience.

So has retirement become a dirty word? People in the City all want to make their millions by the time they are, say, 40, and then have a 'real' life. All they are retiring from is the grind, the stress, the tedium of those deeply extrinsically, but not very intrinsically motivating jobs.

The boundary between work and leisure, between vocation and vacation, between career and post-career is blurring. And so it should.

Many people are more amused than relieved by getting a bus pass or a special heating allowance. They eschew pipe and slippers, rocker, the allotment, and the homely image their parents had.

Retirement is a state of mind, not a calendar date. It's not the end phase of the journey, but another phase of the journey. It's not to be ashamed of. But it needs repackaging. We have senior citizens, oldies, retirees, and veterans. But none of this renaming really captures the nature of the beast.

The cost of this to ourselves and our country means we will have to keep going longer. But many of us do not look at this with fear and dread. Yes, there are jobs no old or young person relishes—traffic warden, or trash collector. There are jobs one has to be fit, dexterous, and alert enough to do well, which may put a ceiling on age.

But there are many jobs in the burgeoning services industry that give a retired person something to do, a structure to their day, a little pocket money, a group of friends, a sense of purpose. In this sense jobs prolong rather than shorten lives.

The anatomy of derailment

Management derailment is a serious issue. High flyers hit turbulence. Anointed wunderkinds seem to have the propensity to derail, fall off the cliff, fail to deliver business.

Figures on derailment are hard to come by. They are hidden, a bit like suicide statistics. But most people know, or know of, stable, able, and seemingly capable managers who lose the plot. It used to be called having a nervous breakdown. Then it was work-induced stress. Now it is called business derailment.

Derailment is multi-faceted and serious debilitation. It can, and, does affect the mental and physical health of executives as well as their colleagues and family. All those connected to the derailer feel the impact.

The question, of course, is what the causes and cures of derailment might be. Many people think, rather forgivingly, and perhaps naively, that derailed managers are simply victims of excessive stress caused by unrealistic and overwhelming job demands that overpower their capacity to fulfill them. But a breakdown and derailment are different. We may all be vulnerable to breakdowns, albeit that they may be neither too acute nor chronic.

Derailment suggests that individuals have personal characteristics—often negative—that may be overlooked, forgiven or not, and that then cause serious problems. It is stress that may trigger the behavioral manifestations of these problems and lead to derailment.

So what are the more typical issues, expressed in non-psychobabble? Many people talk about the *micro-managing control freak*. It is a common problem. This is an anxiety-based disorder that can have many causes. As one rises up the organization one has to do more managing and less supervising, and then more leading and less managing. Work becomes more about the big picture, strategy, and productivity. It's more cerebral and more risky. But it may be hard to let go the previous stage and pattern of work behavior.

You promote people because they are good at their job, but expect them to do a different one. Some are more cut out for the hands-off stuff. Micro-managers can't let go. They seem unable to trust others. They often believe, erroneously, that there is only one way to do something … and it is their own way.

Micro-managers derail because they forget what they are supposed to be doing. They don't trust others to do the job properly and in their own way.

A second cause is the *low integrity, manipulative monster*. These are the conscience-free, borderline psychopaths of the business world. They do anything to get their own way. They lie, cheat, steal, and know how to manipulate others. Hence they can be very charming when they want to be. They are particularly problematic when both intelligent and good-looking.

Charming manipulators know precisely how to get on in business. They know how to flatter and threaten; how to be victim or victimizer; how to ingratiate and intimidate to get their way. The political and backstabbing battleground of most business life is the ideal playground for these individuals.

But at least in the storybooks they get their comeuppance. They do get discovered and exposed by a long line of people they have abused. When they derail it is often with spectacular and lethal consequences.

A third cause is *self-important, egocentric narcissism*. The paradox is that high self-esteem is thought to be a good thing in life. As is looking after your own interests and taking care of yourself.

But a major task of all managers is helping to achieve goals through others. By target setting, continuous support (emotional, informational, social), and regular specific and honest feedback, managers can, should, and must, achieve a great deal. But they are too concerned with their own needs, their personal future, their pathway to the top; it is not long before their staff feel lost, ignored, and forgotten.

Of course, there are other causes. Some derail as a result of their desperately low emotional intelligence; others because they are too slow (or unwilling) to learn and adapt. Some simply focus on the wrong things.

But case studies, personal experience, and theory suggest there are some pretty common factors. So when you meet the charming, self-confident manager who is eager to be hands on, look out. They might have too much of a good thing. Beware the mask of competence. There may be something very different lurking behind it.

The business beauty parade

Both public and private organizations tender for business. Tendering can be conducted in many ways and, often, a very formal and rigid procedure needs to occur to comply with company rules.

Tendering is seen as a highly efficient process. Interested parties have to compete to win lucrative contracts. And competition is at the heart of innovation, cost-efficiency, and the capitalist ethic.

Those who have to evaluate the various applications do so in a variety of ways. Some organizations try to make it easier for themselves by having pre- and proscribed rules for completing applications. In short, the 'application form' design makes for easier comparisons. Others believe this stifles creativity, and allow for a totally flexible form and process.

Again, some are happy to make the judgments entirely by document, be it old-fashioned paper or electronic means. But many wait to see the people behind the proposal. They want to get a sense of who they are; to see if there is chemistry; to see if their faces fit. So they arrange a beauty parade. These may happen at the beginning or end of the process. The parade might be the first filter, or alternatively it might be the way the final judgment is made.

Usually the tendering groups are given a reasonable brief and asked to pitch up for their 'song and dance.' To help the comparison process and to maximize efficiency the selectors try to arrange them on the same day. So the tenderers are given, say, an hour (often much less) to appear before a selection committee. The committee can and does ask questions. It may, indeed *should*, contain people with various types of expertise and various forms of investment in the project. There are many stakeholders in big projects and it is sensible to have them all represented. Disinterested, expert outsiders may also be asked to attend.

With as many as five to nine groups tendering, the selection process can last a couple of days. But the amounts spent easily justify thorough probing of the tenderers' capabilities, intended processes, and costs.

The selection committee may have elaborate, detailed, and sophisticated criteria and processes for making the decision. Or they may rely more heavily on gut feeling. Much has been written on how bad decisions are made by falling into various traps. But what advice to give the beauty-paraders themselves?

- First, before even reading the instructions carefully, do your homework. Try to find out if there are any hidden agendas. Explore, by all means, possible the motives, preferred outcomes, and the intentions of the company beforehand. This might involve telephoning people for 'clarification,' or researching the company's recent history, and so on. Find out not *what* the potential client wants done, but *why*. This may involve imaginative use of sources within and outside the organization.
- Second, establish who on the selection board wants what and who has most power. There is a dynamic to these boards, and their members can be very political and distrustful of one another. Pleasing one person may therefore deeply antagonize another. So make sure you know who are the most important, powerful, and persuasive, and target them.
- Third, follow your instructions, both on paper and in the parade, scrupulously. You may think it trivial but it's the first test. If they ask you to present for 20 minutes don't go over the limit. If they ask you to

address certain questions, do so. It's tempting to play to your strengths, use your favorite presentations and stories, but resist.

- Fourth, don't badmouth others. Concentrate on what you are good at and can do. Don't over-promise, don't rest on your laurels, and don't seem smug and complacent. Schadenfreude and 'tall poppy syndrome' often see the big boys fall first. Be upbeat, positive, and clear.
- Fifth, listen very carefully to the questions. Ask for clarification if necessary. Remember it is likely every group gets the same semi-tricky questions. They are testing how quick you are on your feet, how you can deal with inconsistency, incongruity, and ambiguity. Indeed, try to anticipate the questions and think through some answers.
- Sixth, remember not to contradict what you said in the written bit, or indeed what appears on your website. Committees are sensitive to that sort of thing.
- Seventh, as in all interviews they may offer you an opportunity to ask questions. Prepare these very carefully. Design them as much to flatter as to get genuine information.

There is a psychology of beauty parade success. It's not a case of the 'best man' or even 'who dares wins.' It is those who do their homework and understand committee dynamics that triumph … along, of course, with a pretty good and economical proposal.

The F-word

Is it fair? People at work are, quite naturally, highly sensitive to being treated fairly. Complaints about lack of fairness are ubiquitous. Performance management systems, mergers and acquisitions, and selection methods are all frequently attacked for not being *fair*.

Fairness is about equity, about justice, about being treated appropriately with respect to effort and ability at work, *and* relative the effort of others. Fairness is often a social comparison process whereby we judge our rewards (and punishments) not in absolute terms but in comparative terms. Perceived fairness and justice is a very, very hot button at work, at home, and everywhere.

But there may be quite different types of perceived fairness. If you search the interesting cross-disciplinary work, there appear to be at least four quite different types of issue around what is called organizational justice.

The first is perhaps the hottest. It is called *distributive fairness*. It is about comp and ben: effectively how the spoils are distributed. This is usually and mainly about pay, as that is usually the most obvious output variable and social comparator. But there are numerous other factors, like office dimensions or parking lot space, vacation allowances, promotion, and training opportunities.

Everyone at work has a 'package.' It is what they receive in return for their work, service, loyalty, etc. And employees are enormously sensitive to the packages of others inside the organization. Some things are easier to compare than others. Because people don't usually speak honestly to each other about the details of their packages, we have to guess. Some organizations try to prevent social comparison by keeping things secret; others try the totally transparent approach.

The problem lies in the fact that peers are acutely aware of each other's work styles, productivity, and cooperativeness. Work with a slow, unhelpful, frequently absent person and you know the burden you carry. And if that individual is paid the same as you (when you perceive yourself to be cooperative, dedicated, and productive) you feel (very) unfairly dealt with. Equal distribution is seen to be fair when, and only when, work effort and outcome are equal.

Next there is *procedural fairness*. This is essentially how fairness decisions are made. What processes and procedures are in place to make distribution decisions? Are the procedures transparent or opaque? Are they PR flim-flan or serious business? How does one 'price' a new job? How are redundancy and early retirement packages determined? What rules are followed? Is it LIFO (last in, first out) or FIFO (first in, first out)? Is service and seniority rated above productivity?

Organizations have rules and procedures. They emanate from very different parts of the organization. Some come from the board or finance. Many of the F-sensitive ones are located in HR. These are the people who do all that semi- or non-statutory stuff on paternity leave, flexible working, and space allocation.

The third is *interpersonal fairness*. It's how people are treated on a day-to-day basis. Everyone likes to be treated with dignity, respect, and sensitivity. We all want a boss (and peers) with emotional intelligence. We like our bosses to be self-aware, skilful, resilient, inspirational, and competent. And we do not like them to have favorites. We do not like them to be moody, irascible, and rude. Everyone suffers from stress at some time. The question is whether that stress is passed on; whether people are unfairly blamed or harassed or put upon because of the frustrations of their boss.

The final issue is sometimes called *informational fairness*. This is about whether the information one receives at work is both sufficient and accurate. It is an issue first of quantity, and next of quality. Most people believe their boss has at least one secret that concerns them and that is not communicated to them. Do a climate survey and you always get the same answer: there is a problem with communication. People say they do not get enough accurate and salient information about their jobs and their future.

People need information to do their job. They need clear goals and feedback on how they are doing. They need all that SMART stuff (Specific, Measurable, Achievable, Realistic, Trackable). They also need a mechanism, or a channel, for upward feedback. What they need and want are opportunities and the means to give and receive information that is important to their job.

Block a channel or hide facts and you get gossip, the grapevine, and whistle-blowers. Perceived fairness is pretty complex, then. And it's pretty important. Obviously, some people are particularly fairness-sensitive. But no one ignores the issue. Most of the F—ing at work is actually about fairness.

The joy of shopping

There are more shopaphiles than shopaphobes. And there does appear to be a sex difference in shopping preferences and predilections. Something to do with Venus and Mars, if you are prone to all the socio-biology stuff.

In their book on sex differences (*Why Men Don't Listen and Women Can't Read Maps*), Allan and Barbara Pease say, quite forwardly and unabashed by their datalessness, that women can and do shop in an 'unstructured way,' for no definite outcome. Males, whose need is to make a quick kill and take it home, need a target and a timetable. They believe men can be motivated to shop only if given clear criteria for the purchase (brand, style, color, size), a map of or directions to where to shop, even criteria for how long they should be at it!

People do spend a lot of time at malls and in stores. Now they spend hours surfing the web shopaholically. But what are their motives? Are there clearly different types based on different reasons for shopping?

Over 30 years ago the marketing chaps tried to offer a list of motives. One researcher had a typology of 16 fundamental human motivations, suggesting that shopping behavior arises for three fundamental reasons: to acquire a product, to acquire both a desired product and provide satisfaction with non-product-related needs, or primarily to attain goals not related to product acquisition. These fundamental shopping motives were captured in seven dimensions of shopping motivation labeled 'anticipated utility,' 'role enactment,' 'negotiation,' 'choice optimization,' 'affiliation,' 'power/authority' and 'stimulation.'

But, more recently, the retailing analysts have identified six clear, different 'hedonic shopping motives.'

1. *Adventure shopping*: shopping is seen as an exciting adventure. Shopping offers a sensory world of new sights, sounds, and smells. Stores are like adventure playgrounds. They provide a marvelous source of stimulation.

2. *Social shopping*: this is the bonding shopping experience. It is a way to spend time with friends and family. Perhaps that is why there are so many places to eat and drink in stores these days. Shopping can help people express their altruistic, cohesive, and acceptance needs. Shopping with others can be just like any other social activity: some go once a week to evening school, others to badminton, and some go shopping together.

3. *Gratification shopping*: this is more akin to retail therapy. It is shopping for stress relief, shopping to indulge, shopping to pick oneself up. For some it's winding down, while for others it is a distraction. Quite clearly it is all about escapism, neo-therapeutic self-gratification. Some now call it an emotion-focused coping strategy.

4. *Idea shopping*: the fashion conscious and presumably fashion victims in particular have to find a way to keep up with what is new. They need to know what is in and what is not. There are trends in everything from boys' toys to girls' fashions. Stores are a laboratory, a catalogue, a library, and an exhibition all rolled into one. The shopper is essentially a researcher.

5. *Role shopping*: shopping for others can be, for some, deeply satisfying and gratifying. People feel good about gift shopping. It allows them to act out their role of parent, friend, admirer, lover, and the like. It has become a way to enact and fulfill culturally prescribed roles in our society.

6. *Value shopping*: this is the discount-seeking bargain hunter who sees the whole shopping experience as a challenge and a game to be won. These shoppers are

competitive achievers out to seek increased self-esteem and the admiration of their peers.

So shopping is a thrill-seeking adventure, a major social occasion, a mood enhancer, a trend-setting research expedition, a relationship builder, and a bargain hunt. Shopping can provide 'flow'—that optimal experience of being totally engrossed. It can distort time and hours can pass without notice. The sheer aesthetic beauty of the stores can make shopping uplifting.

Of course, the trouble with all typologies, or even dimensions, is that they offer an irresistible temptation to the obsessional to split one category, add another, or combine two or more. Few people fit neatly into each box. But it is a start.

The question, of course, is what are the implications for retailers? Advertising can be targeted at the different shopping types. Some are attracted by price, others by novelty, and others still by variety. Stores can and have introduced certain features because they recognize their various predominant market types. So we have the bookstore-café concept, the discovery-science store, and the privilege card after-hours evening.

Stores might like to investigate the motives of their repeat customers. These motives may be linked to gender, age, social class, and ethnicity. It may help to understand the current group as well as attract new hedonic types.

And if retailers understand their clients they should see an increase in such desirable things as satisfaction, loyalty, and profit.

The narcissism business

Vanity is a great motivator. The British honors system of patronage may have innumerable detractors, but it certainly motivates a good deal of charity work, not to mention party donations.

But the commercial world has not been slow in exploiting this most deep-seated and darkest of needs. One growing manifestation is the *Who's Who* business.

The original red book, *Who's Who,* is a flourishing British institution that started in 1849. It is subtitled *An Annual Biographical Dictionary* and contains over 30,000 entries. Everyone 'in the know' in Britain is clear about the signs of having made it in life: a decent gong, a *Who's Who* entry, or an invitation to appear on BBC Radio 4's *Desert Island Discs* and choose one's favorite music. Of course, a hat trick of obits in the broadsheets is much desired, but one is unlikely to appreciate it fully!

Who's Who is *the* list of the eminent. How you are chosen is a mystery: strangely comforting to those who have crossed the barrier and remain in 'for life', and deeply frustrating for those who don't know why they have not been selected. Periodically there are witch hunts; investigative journalism attempts to find out how the system works.

The result: the ins and not-ins; the quietly smug and the outrageously discriminated against. It is a deep wound against pride; even vanity; perhaps narcissism.

And seeing a need, in tiptoe the entrepreneurs. Why should there be only one *Who's Who*? Don't like the system? Start your own. There is surely a large army of people eager to sign up for inclusion and buy—at outrageous prices— thick books full of thousands upon thousands of never-made-its hungry for recognition.

As a nation of self-esteem enthusiasts the Americans got into this game first. Now, Britain, that old Imperial power who invents everything but has to be taught how to exploit those inventions, is catching up fast.

Who's Who has proliferated to meet the apparently insatiable demand to have one's achievements acknowledged. People in the headlines, and many who are not, will attest to being bombarded by offers to appear in yet another of these weighty tomes.

They come in essentially three forms. There is the *Who's Who in Nowhereville* approach. This is done by geographic region. And of course driven by demand. Areas are getting smaller: soon you may come across *Who's Who in North Swindon* or the *Isle of Dogs Who's Who*.

A second type is the *Who's Who* by 'achievement area.' So we can have *Who's Who* in science or medicine, engineering or manufacturing. Of course, the guy who runs the local chemist may feel he deserves mention in them all. But if he and others like him want to appear, they'll just have to wait for *Who's Who in Retail Pharmaceuticals*.

The third type is the brashly alternative book that eschews the words *Who's Who* and goes for titles like *International Biographies of Achievement*, or some such.

The clues to the nature of the enterprise and the narcissism that it feeds are two-fold. First, just when the letter of congratulation on the wonderful achievements and a lifetime of service arrives, so does an order form for the book. Two things are noticeable. The cost is often very high, usually starting at $300-plus. And, given that people may be squashed 20 to the page, that's a lot for a moment of glory. Next, the book always comes in various forms: bog standard, but nevertheless very expensive; leather-bound; gold-embossed, etc. This means the book is a record, a trophy, a treasure for all time. So why not cough up the extra for a pig-skinned, fine old craftsman, parchment paper edition?

The second, even more obvious, giveaway is the 'mention a friend' section. This is usually dressed up as 'assist our researchers' but means in effect 'Do you know some gullible vain person like yourself?' The problem with this, of course, is that it reduces exclusivity. Half the thrill of being in a *Who's Who* is knowing that your friends are not.

All this may be a sign of that most common and dangerous of personality disorders: narcissism. It is a potential derailer but, paradoxically, narcissism can serve business people very well.

So what are the markers of narcissism? The narcissistic manager is marked by grandiosity (in fantasy or behavior), need for admiration, and lack of empathy. Self-centered, selfish, egotistical: narcissists are everywhere in business.

- They have a grandiose sense of self-importance (e.g. exaggerated achievements and talents, expectation to be recognized as superior without commensurate achievements).
- Most are preoccupied with fantasies of unlimited success, power, brilliance, and money.
- They believe that they are 'special' and unique, and can only be understood by, or should associate with, other special or high-status people (or institutions). They may try to 'buy' themselves into exclusive circles.
- They require excessive admiration and respect from everyone at work. Always.
- Bizarrely, they often have a sense of entitlement (i.e. unreasonable expectations of favorable treatment or automatic compliance with their manifest needs). Worse, they take advantage of others to achieve their own ends, which makes them terrible managers.
- They lack empathy. All are unwilling to recognize or identify with the feelings and needs of others. They have desperately low EQ.

- Curiously, they are often envious of others and believe that others are envious of them.
- They show arrogant, haughty behaviors or attitudes all the time and everywhere at work (and home). At times this can be pretty amusing, but is mostly simply frustrating.

Narcissism is full-blown vanity. Narcissists want to buy *Who's Who* rather than merely appear in it. But the journey from ambition to narcissism may not be that long. And the line between arrogance, vanity, and narcissism is a thin one.

Beware bright, good-looking, ambitious narcissists. They are very dangerous. For them, all business is the narcissism business.

The office party

The office outing, the summer barbie, and the Christmas party are (or perhaps were) markers in the business year. They might be a time for fun and games, for Mardi Gras, for families. They were judged to be good for morale and therefore cost-effective.

But times have changed. Religious sensitivities, the PC police, insurance costs, and the grey men of the bottom line have all conspired against the office party.

Some say Christmas parties offend people of all faiths, including devout Christians who see nothing religious in them. Others get worried about 'under the mistletoe behavior,' or reports of shrieks from the stationery store room last year. And it is getting more expensive, particularly if a non-office venue is hired and families brought along.

Some say they become 'partied out' at Christmas and are glad to have one fewer to worry about. Others complain that they are all deeply embarrassed to see the CEO trying to dance with young support staff, or the head of marketing being dressed up as Santa Claus, or a rock star in a pantomime. Those concerned by binge drinking and drink-driving see the summer barbie as the source of terrible temptations that lead to accidents.

And yet a party is cheery celebration, particularly in the dead of winter. It can be seen as a sign of thanks for hard work, as an opportunity to meet and mix with people outside one's silo, and as a way of marking a significant point in the year.

Certainly there are problems at Christmas, but a few simple rules can help measures. *First*, there are the gift-giving rules. Whether you give individual gifts to others or put in and draw them from a 'grotto,' there needs to be a clear and explicit limit on cost (say $20). Gift-giving is a reciprocal business and people can feel inadequate, or 'bought,' if given a gift they cannot reciprocate.

Second, it may be that certain gifts are 'off the menu.' These are jokes that backfire. *Third*, better make them androgynous than strongly gender-related. Hence useful little objects like key fobs that can be used by all.

The summer party, too, has rules. They probably relate to dress as much as anything else, particularly if there is a swimming pool involved. The sight of a sexually provocative temp revealing far too much flesh to goggle-eyed middle-aged middle managers just won't do.

There is always an issue about the entertainment if there is to be any. In the old days it was not only acceptable but almost required for the 'little people' to have a shot at the 'big people.' Gently yes, with grace and good humor, but nevertheless accurate. That's not so clear any more.

And, of course, there is now the horror of litigation. If someone drinks too much and has an accident on their way home, who is to blame? If burns occur to their mouth or fingers from a hot dog at the barbie, who picks up the tab? So there may be insurance costs ... prohibitively high insurance costs.

It is becoming so complicated and so expensive that the office party might be in danger of extinction, like the village bonfire or the church fete. We are forced to have fewer, less jolly, and less frequent non-work get-togethers. The work of anti-social, avaricious spoilsports, or at last the introduction of safety rules and procedures designed to protect all? Discuss ... on your next works outing.

The package

It is not only job seekers, those made redundant, and the disenchanted who read the job ads. Naturally, head-hunters, HR, PR and IR people, and strategists read the appointments or job market section of newspapers and magazines. These pages can reveal which sectors are expanding, which key jobs seem troublesome to fill, and where turnover is high.

But even the contented middle-aged, middle-brow, middle manager has been known to ponder over job advertisements. This social comparison process can stir powerful emotions of anger and envy or quiet satisfaction. Ads from your own organization are particularly useful for social comparison processes.

What do the job ads tell you? Most start off by saying what a wonderful opportunity has arisen to work for this world-class, successful, go-ahead company. After that, there's some description of the job: the role, the accountabilities, the essential task.

Then there are the desired attributes, competencies, or personality traits. What is essentially surprising about these is that they are almost always identical and frequently positively coded. So you need energy, focus, commercial acumen, vision, passion, creativity, empathy, charisma, and all those leadership, people, and analytical skills we read about. They are the same for almost every job, it seems.

So you know where the job is located, who the employer is, and the job title. The job description and role may be rather vague and the requirements pretty ambitious, but what you need to know, yet are not told, is the precise salary.

HR people talk of a package rather than a salary. And there is that quaint concept called 'compensation and benefits.' The package—often not easily or radically negotiable—may contain all manner of features one does or possibly does not want.

Part of the comp and ben may be a car and private medical insurance. It might be shares or discounts on products. It may involve an entertainment or travel or housing allowance. These features differ from place to place and time to time.

So the package is made up of many things. Never under-estimate the value of the job title. To be director of HR is different from head of HR, who reports to the director. There is the length of contract to consider. There is the distance to work and the public transport available. More importantly then ever, there are the pension arrangements.

Packages are complex and often problematic. Some aspects are negotiable and others are not. Some features are highly desirable and others are not. Some items are known to the selectors and others are not. Some things are discussable and others are not.

Most packages involve a trade-off and the salary is only one component. US companies may offer only half the vaca-tion allowance of German firms, but better opportunities. Some jobs offer frequent exciting business travel, but this can soon pall. Some talk about, but others really offer, the possi-bility of working at home and the work–life balance thing.

Package attractiveness is a function of age and stage. It's a function of ego and ambition. The cash-rich, time-poor know the value of vacations. In this sense the same package can seem either very attractive or unattractive to two individ-uals.

Trade-off is a balancing act. Some people like the list approach, where you have two columns to fill: the pluses and the minuses. And with a simple bit of arithmetic we can decide to 'go for' a job, or not.

But there are three problems with this reasonable, rational

approach. *First,* much of the most important data is not in the ads. And it may not even be known to those at the selection committee. In this sense there is a lot of missing data before beginning.

Second, advertisements are just that. They need decoding. They may be little more than company PR. Thus 'challenging' means 'stressful', 'energy' means 'exhausting,' 'analytic' means 'rocket science.' They don't say the job may soon be regraded after restructuring. They don't say that none of the previous incumbents lasted more than a year. They don't say morale is at rock bottom. You can't and shouldn't expect them to. But it makes the calculations difficult.

Third, things change fast in business. Even if the candidate has full information and reasonable calculative skills, jobs change. Companies are bought up. Sudden geopolitical and technical change can have high impacts. But that's life.

The moral of the story? Jobs are more than title, salary, and location. It's important to examine the cost–benefit analysis of all aspects of the job. And if you can't tell, get on the web or the phone, and sniff about. It is always wise to do one's homework to prevent disillusion, derailment, and disaster.

The paradox of new products

Many organizations are in awe of creativity and its close cousin, innovation. They know they live in a rapidly changing, complex world. They know they have to adapt or die. But they chase something more than that: the brilliant new idea and product that will bring sudden massive success and fame.

The belief is that customers want the new and improved model. Not just an adaptation of a previous version but something *radically* new. They want the breakthrough in design, functionality, etc. Sometimes this is a serious scientific or technical leap, as is often the case with drugs or IT, and sometimes it is through a quirky genius working in his shed at home.

There are many stories of the millions made by individuals and companies on the basis of one very bright idea. Correspondingly, disastrous products are not quickly forgotten or overlooked. So the hunt is on for the holy grail: the innovative product to delight.

How, then, to get creativity and innovation in the organization? Seek out creative people in recruitment and selection? Make creativity a competency to be rewarded? Send current employees to creativity workshops? Bring in humor or creativity consultants? Have a creative artist or scientist in residence?

The whole mania for novelty is based on the premise that customers actually *want* something different, as opposed to something they know, like, and trust. A creative product is defined by the dual criteria of new and useful. But to what extent does the average customer want creative novelty? If they do, in what particular area and what particular type of product?

Consider the typical purchases made at supermarkets, department stores and, increasingly, on the web. How often is one seeking something new or something tried and trusted?

How many organizations have lost out by replacing a successful product with a new innovative one? Remember Coca-Cola? Granted, with change there is almost always an initial resistance, but if the product is of genuine benefit, it will sell. Most often people don't have choice. The old product is withdrawn, the new one substituted, like it or lump it.

Only those utterly ignorant of statistical sampling methods would require both old and new available for a reasonable period of time to enable assessment of frequency of purchase of each item. Sales figures would then be plotted. Ideally, the profile of the purchasers would also be logged. Is it the young, socially upwardly mobile, and technologically literate who choose the new product, and the down-at-heel, poor, and technologically illiterate who choose the old?

But how much does the average customer like change and innovation in products? Changing advertising or changing packaging is one issue, but changing the contents is quite another. Even something superficial like product packaging color can put off the customer. People get used to the characteristics of certain brands: their smell, feel, and packaging. They like its quirkiness, which is why some brands have never changed (Angostura Bitters, for example) even if they look strikingly old-fashioned. Indeed, that may be their precise appeal.

The problem often lies in the different perspectives of suppliers and buyers. Suppliers, be they R&D boffins or marketing people, really live their brand. For them it is a unique, live object. They know the history and are often obsessed by its unique story. Suppliers are in the business of differentiation between themselves and their competition.

And they innovate to preserve this uniqueness, particularly when others muscle in on their territory.

But how do things look from the customer's perspective? Do they buy white goods, or computers, or even food-stuffs because of their uniqueness or specialty? Who knows or cares about the multiple functions on most electronic goods, which are neither understood nor used? Who cares about nifty compartments or crafty widgets? The R&D, marketing, and ad people do, but does the customer?

In many instances customers' needs are refreshingly simple. They buy a category of goods, not a brand. They want a fair price, reliability, and good service. They want something they know and can trust rather than always the new improved model that offers functions and deign they do not like, want, or understand.

The psychology of gossip and the grapevine

However smart and smooth the 'internal communications department', gossip thrives in organizations, particularly those in trouble. Glossy in-house (staff) magazines, a monthly video talk from the CEO, and regular email communication can neither prevent nor even inhibit the work of the grapevine. Often the attempt to formalize, control, and sanitize all communication within an organization really backfires. It is seen as window-dressing, propaganda, and little more than PR for senior managers. Gossip is trusted, fun, and, it seems, endemic.

In his socio-biologically inspired book *Managing the Human Animal*, Nigel Nicholson from the London Business School argues that we are hard-wired to appreciate gossip. Business gossip, he argues, is a sort of interpersonal grooming. In the process people are able to establish where they are in the hierarchy, who the key people at work are, what threats and opportunities lie on the horizon, as well as keeping up the information highway to one another, and signifying that the other person is valuable and important.

Gossip is the glue of networks. It is a bonding mechanism. And, of course, it serves to make up for all the incompetencies of the formal internal stuff. Rumors are trusted more than official communiqués because the latter are all too often censored, late, and distorted.

So much for the business take. What is the psychology of gossip?

Ubiquitous and unacceptable, gossip has a long history because it serves such important functions. In the Bible, both

Ecclesiastes and Leviticus warn against it. It is the destroyer of relationships and reputations, a hubble-bubble cauldron of trouble.

The dictionary emphasizes the light, trivial, and trifling nature of gossip. It also specifies the negative aspect—the groundless rumor, the tittle-tattle, the evidence-free idle talk.

Gossip varies according to the type of gossip, the number of gossipers, the status of the gossiper and, perhaps surprisingly, the credibility (legitimacy) of the gossiper.

Get on your ethical high-horse and gossip of all kinds is *unequivocally morally indefensible*. Gossipers are purveyors of misinformation, bursting with envy, pusillanimity, and venom.

How common is it? Well, that depends on the definition. A pretty inclusive definition is that gossip is the producing, hearing, or otherwise participating in evaluative comment about someone not present. It means spreading rumors, telling tales, or talking behind people's backs. Of course, one can make interesting academic distinctions between malicious gossip and salacious gossip. Between 'idle' gossip and goal-oriented gossip. Between accurate and inaccurate gossip.

But it's pretty common. Given the above definition, researchers estimate that as much as 70 percent of conversation time at work involves gossip.

Most agree that a necessary, if not sufficient, definition of gossip is that a *third party*, indeed the very focus of the activity, *is not present*. It is all about A talking to B about C, who is not there. You can't gossip about yourself. You can disclose things about yourself and guess what others are saying about you, but self-gossip is oxymoronic.

Gossip is colorful, evaluative, and has valence. In short, it is juicy. It can be hagiographically positive or demoniacally negative. It is deeply value laden. You have praising gossip and blaming gossip. Anointing and assassinating gossip.

Virtual, spiral or vicious circle, gossip. It is rarely bland, factual, or disinterested.

The *content* of the conversation is not the only factor that distinguishes it. You need the right setting for gossip, the atmosphere, the peculiarly 'licensed' conditions for the activity. A gossip-friendly, gossip-inducing, gossip-accepting situation is one of intimacy and intrigue, gusto and gutsiness, drama and bedevilment.

Gossip exists because it has serious social functions. It creates group solidarity by facilitatory information.

Curiously, gossip is both an efficient and exclusive means of gathering and disseminating information. It is the inside scoop versus the official line. It is useful, timely, even rare currency. Gossipers have status—their access to, and understanding of, information is pretty important. They control a scarce resource. It has exchange value.

Gossip is, above all, entertainment. It is unalloyed fun. It is a bulwark against monotony. It is storytelling and recreational.

Sharing gossip builds and secures bonds. It brings people together, establishes boundaries. It sets the limits of the clan, culture, and tribe. You have to be an insider to appreciate and deal in gossip. Insiders are trusted with and appreciate gossip; outsiders are simply excluded.

Gossip can be enormously influential. It can cut down the tall poppy, it can police freeloaders and social cheats, it can praise and shame.

Gossip is often the way corporate cultures are established and maintained. Corporate cultures are about mores and norms, formal and informal rules, and who breaks them. Gossip pricks pompous balloons. It is the antidote to spin, to inaccurate impression management, to PR.

The subjects of gossip sometimes try to so something about it. They might reduce their eccentricities, obey the rules more, or ferret out the gossipers. Often gossipers try simultaneously to hide details of their own lives while exposing those of others.

So gossip may be a benign hobby, a social glue, or a pretension pricker. But is it good for you? Has it an adaptive function? Gossip can be cathartic—it can help to let off steam. But it can also induce guilt. The gossiper is in an ambivalent situation. Gossips try to camouflage their activity and motives by 'letting things slip.'

So gossip has its euphemisms: you 'chew the fat,' 'shoot the breeze,' 'chit-chat,' or 'talk shop.' Doing lunch, or meeting for a drink, may be an acceptable way to meet for gossip.

So is gossip good for you? Well sort of. It can be the most accurate, efficient, and successful channel of useful communications. It has a social and survival function, and a clear utility value. But it can 'eat up' the gossiper in guilt or act as a dangerous and devious conduit of half-truths and distortions.

We are at once morally ambivalent and socially dependent on organizational gossip.

PROTECTING VULNERABLE CUSTOMERS

Frequently on those mildly addictive consumer report TV shows we get reports of unscrupulous people targeting the elderly. The targets tend to have certain things in common: they live alone, they are middle class, and they are relatively easily parted from their money. They tend to be trusting and some appear to have rather a lot of senior moments.

The perpetration of the offence of abusing vulnerable customers comes in many shapes and sizes. Not all fit the rogue builder image of paunch and tattoo. Many are well-dressed, quasi-professionals, selling everything from financial products to household goods.

Old people are, like all of us, sold things by cold-callers on the telephone as well as on the doorstep. And they, too, are told that they have won spectacular prizes that are, of course, bogus. We all need to be aware of the latest scam.

The issue of exploiting the vulnerable is one of increasing importance. People are living longer. Older people often have fairly large sums of disposable, or at least accessible, income. Manufacturers are now interested in providing various expensive gadgets and goods that increase or facilitate mobility (stairlifts or electric scooters) as well as products to make things more comfortable (special chairs and beds).

So how to protect the vulnerable? Certainly this has become the focus of court cases, which will no doubt increase. Various groups have been working on these issues, like Thomas Bayne of Mountainview, a London-based consultancy. He, and his colleagues, have tried to understand the nature of vulnerability and help companies devise sales-related policies to ensure they do not infringe the law or good ethical practice.

Like all weak essays, but clearly out of necessity, one really needs to start with a definition. What does it mean to be vulnerable, as in a customer that is vulnerable, or easily exploited by high-pressure sales techniques?

There are two problems with arriving at a straightforward working definition: the first is that vulnerability clearly lies on a continuum from 'Not at all' to 'Very,' and one has the near impossible task of drawing a pretty simple line in the sand. Next, of course, there are different dimensions of vulnerability. Indeed four can readily be distinguished.

1. *Comprehension vulnerability*: this is essentially about understanding what one is being sold, at what price, and under what conditions. It is related to many factors, like education, intelligence, mother tongue, culture, and age. Many people claim they did not understand the contract document they signed, meaning that they did not fully or sufficiently comprehend what they were told or sold, and all the subtle and terribly important ramifications of the sale. Indeed, as we know, 'what the big print giveth, the small print taketh away.' Older people have problems of hearing, or failing short-term memory. Many may have had little contact with and hence little understanding of financial language. This problem is compounded if their first language is not (in this case) English, or if they come from a culture where the 'rules' of selling are very different. This is always compounded by home selling as there are many complex rules about treating strangers in the home. Older, politer, more trusting people from another era may feel much less certain about 'seeing off' unwelcome callers to their home.

   Comprehension vulnerability can be tested for. It's a good study for a psycho-gerontologist or a cognitive psychologist. But we know the groups from which these people are most likely to come and we can devise safeguards to protect them.

2. *Financial vulnerability*: lots of people are effectively financially illiterate, or irresponsible, or troubled. They very easily get into debt. They buy on the 'never-never.' They readily buy things they really cannot afford and undertake regular repayments they can, in no way, realistically serve over any period of time. Many do not understand the arithmetic of interest rates. They may be unwilling, unused to, or unable to save to make better financial arrangements. Furthermore, they may not

understand the possibilities of 'haggling' for discounts and the like. The financially vulnerable tend to be less educated, although this does not apply to all, of course. They are often detectable through a history of repossessions or problematic credit records.

3. *Physical vulnerability*: many people suffer from various forms of sensory or motor impairment. They may not see or hear well, and have difficulty getting about. They may, as a consequence, be particularly vulnerable in their own homes where they feel unable to eject people. Physical vulnerability naturally affects comprehension vulnerability. And it increases with age. Essentially the issue is that one or more disabilities affect(s) a person's ability to make reasonable decisions. They can't fully inspect goods, they cannot read small print, or they do not hear all the information they are being given.

4. *Assertiveness vulnerability*: this concerns having the social skills associated with all negotiations. It means feeling comfortable and confident in simply saying 'no' without shame, embarrassment, or incoherence. There are countless cases of people buying things they really did not want because they did not know how to turn away an experienced and subtle salesperson, who fully understands how to manipulate emotions, break rules, exploit cultural norms of reciprocity, and such like.

There may be other types of vulnerability (or other words to describe it) but the above seem to capture most of the issues. Of course, they are all related and some groups may be particularly vulnerable. However, it is no doubt the first type of vulnerability—comprehension—that is the most fundamental. It is also where good companies and the law can intervene.

So how can you make sure you are not abusing the comprehension vulnerable by selling people something they may have wanted, but who did not understand the cost and conditions and consequences of the contract? It's not practical to give them an intelligence, hearing, or credit-worthiness test.

But there are things selling organizations can, and should,

do if they sell to potentially vulnerable customers. First, take account of the selling situation. Where is it taking place, what are the social norms and conventions, how much pressure is coming to bear on the individual? The dentist's chair may be a good example of a place where it is harder to make good decisions.

But there are sensible and sensitive checks and balances that can relatively easily be put in place when booking or confirming a sales appointment. This provides an excellent opportunity to ask a few unobtrusive questions, which may help identify the comprehension vulnerable. They are, of course, not as crude as those well-known precursor-to-sectioning questions like 'What day is it today?' or 'Who is the president?'

One can, to some extent, tell if someone is deaf, or confused, or a non-native speaker struggling with language. But sometimes basic questions can tap into memory and understanding. 'What is the nearest highway or main-line station?' 'What is your full zip code?' 'Have you ever bought any of these (or similar) products before?' 'What day of the week were you born on?' The dates of birth of their spouse, children, wedding, and so on.

What organizations could do when going through a relatively well-thought-through and tested script is to ensure that they are categorizing potential customers in terms of their risk for being comprehension vulnerable. This could be, say, a three- or five-point scale from 'Not at all,' through 'Potentially' to 'Very.'

Any sales person or organization needs to size up their appetite for risk at this point. Risks of court cases, loss of reputation, and the like. It is far better to have a well-thought-through plan and strategy for avoiding the vulnerable consumer and for managing the potentially vulnerable. This may mean asking for a friend or relative to be present at the sales meeting.

It certainly would be a paradox if those companies that do not take full cognizance of the vulnerability of their customers end up themselves being highly vulnerable in the eyes of the law.

The psychology of red tape

For every action there is an opposite or equal reaction. As true in business as it is in physics. This certainly applies to legislation.

There seems to be a type of individual whose natural instinct is to try to impose rules. We'd all like to live in an orderly, just, predictable world. We like to believe that justice wins out, that hard work is equitably rewarded, and that people get a fair deal and a fair shot at the target of life.

But it is conspicuously not so. Often the bad guys win and the meek are deprived of the earth.

There are many reactions for the injustices of the world, be they economic, political, or social. And one reaction is to want to impose rules, edicts, and laws. The idea is to pre- and proscribe 'proper' behavior. Laws and rules supposedly ensure fair play. They attempt (it is hoped) to ensure that people act openly, honorably, and fairly. From a very early age, certain individuals clearly enjoy doing this, even in the playground. Their urge is to order; their means red tape. To some it is simply the curtailment of freedom. Rules inhibit, restrict, and restrain.

Collectively individuals can form together into groups whose needs for standardization, for predictability, and for clarity encourage them to establish a red-tape culture. Red-tapers are made uncomfortable by ambiguity and uncertainty. They are particularly frightened of people doing their own thing. Freedom is akin to anarchy in their view.

To the red-taper, rules bring order *and* fairness. They ensure the collective good is considered and that selfish, amoral people are unable to impose their will on the inno-cent. They bring about a fair, just, and disciplined society. No wonder dictators of both the left and right are so fond of red tape.

The urge to legislate, to impose rules, to bind in red tape is probably normally distributed, like all human characteristics. From this one might divide the population into three groups: extreme *legisphiles*, mild *legisphiles*, and *legisphobes*.

Extreme legisphiles live their lives by their own rules and those of others. They may indeed seek out jobs that are rule-bound. Better still they may seek to find jobs that rejoice in rules and restrictions. Health and safety comes to mind, or local government. They have a love, bordering on the obsessional, of order. And clarifying it to others.

They may enjoy being on ethical committees or juries. They may, over time, become experts on obscure aspects of the law. They may choose to become local councilors, school governors, and the like (though these posts may involve too much wheeler-dealering in pursuit of election).

They have many and varied pet hates. Consider the idea of unallocated seating on low-cost flights. Total anathema to the extreme legisphile, who sees the whole thing as chaotically unfair. In fact, anything to do with deregulation is deeply threatening.

Mild legisphiles prefer that there are national, local, and organizational laws, rules, and requirements. But they do not make a fetish out of it and see them as benevolent attempts to bring about beneficial outcomes. They understand that in times of crisis or trouble like war, terrorism, or financial collapse, more rules and laws are required. They endure; stoically accepting.

And they might, on occasion, even press for the imposition of rules. Driven to distraction by selfish neighbors, unable to work because of unpredictable colleagues, cheated by unethical business people, they may be very happy to support attempts to pass more laws.

The mildly legisphobic grumble a great deal. They see

governments, and more especially in Britain the EU, as over zealous red-tapers. They recall and rejoice in stories about how many new rules have been imposed over the past few years. They distrust bureaucrats and rejoice in the eradication of clause and codicil from complex laws. They probably favored metrication and the removal of layers of government. Devolution, in their eyes, means more bureaucrats. Why have local *and* county councilors, MPs *and* MEPs?

The extreme legisphobics are simmering on the verge of apoplectic rage.

The sales manager

When asked about the worst aspect of their job, a shocking 65–75 percent of employees nominate not pay or customers, nor long hours or lack of promotion prospects, but their immediate boss. One study showed that working for an overbearing boss actually resulted in increased blood pressure in subordinates.

Of course, bad bosses come in various guises. They may be egocentric, rude, disrespectful, and demanding. Equally, they may be pompous fools believing that all their staff (whom they chose) are in fact incompetent and unworthy of promotion or a raise. Some are micro-managers, unable to delegate; others secretive.

Just as it's not difficult to list the characteristics of a bad boss, there is general agreement about what you find in an effective, likeable, preferred boss. Such people tend to be personable, highly emotionally intelligent, and have both an interest in, and ability, to develop others. They tend to be optimistic in seeking win/win solutions. They can adapt and change, and are always flexible. They are self-aware and good communicators.

Most importantly they have integrity as well as vision. They behave consistently over time and treat all colleagues the same. And they do teamwork rather than talk a good game.

It is well known that people from certain occupations can be brilliant technical experts but often make poor managers. It is true of engineering, finance, and information technology. Brilliant, but introverted and convergent-thinking, these individuals are often pretty low on sensitivity and EQ. They may be emotionally illiterate and pretty socially unskilled, having dedicated their formative years to educational rather than social pursuits. So the problem is if and when to promote the technical expert.

But what about those in sales? Natural-born leaders or short-term, superficial charmers? We all know the profile of successful sales staff. They are upbeat and resilient. They are charming and goal oriented. They have energy and are perceptive. And they understand targets. So surely they make good managers?

To promote people out of jobs in which they are both good and happy is always a risk. This may be particularly true of sales staff, paradoxically because they may be financially worse off when promoted. Front-line sales staff have low-base-rate, high-commission remuneration, so that through effort and ability they can make serious cash. But the manager of sales staff sells less and manages more, so may make less money.

On the one hand, there are characteristics that in good sales people spill over to make them good managers. They tend to be good at setting goals and targets, and they tend to be positive.

But, despite their sociability, many sales people have difficulty with teamwork. Many are quirky, rugged individualists, happy doing their own thing in their own way at their own pace. They do one-on-one brilliantly with clients and enjoy the hoopla and banter of a sales conference or post-meeting dinner, but they don't always understand the dynamics of teams and how to shape them.

Sales people may also be both too people oriented and short-term goal oriented to think about strategic planning. It's the marketing branch of 'sales and marketing' that often does the strategy thing. A good strategic plan involves quite a lot of data accumulation and analysis. It is a 'propeller head' number-tumbling activity that may not come easily to some super sales people.

Sales people 'do' vision and enthusiasm and people skills. They tend to be 'sort of' consistent and have 'enough' integrity. But to be a sales manager involves stepping up to a new level. They are not selling to their staff in the same way as they sold to their customers.

It takes a different skill and value set to be a manager compared to a sales person. Some are good at both. But it's daft to take the extremely happy and successful sales person out of the field and dump them in head office where they feel isolated and helpless.

The trick is to know who to 'promote,' and indeed what package to offer them. Extroverted sales people are more sensitive to promise of reward than threat of punishment. They are very sensitive to positive feedback. Hence all the prizes and trinkets they give each other. They are status conscious, competitive, and target-driven. They really value outward, visible signs of success and rank (biggest office, car, desk). So job titles and packages are really important. Not every super sales person makes an excellent, even competent manager. Help people to do well at what they are good at, develop talent when you see it, and make sure promotion out of the line is the best thing for both the individual and the organization.

The trouble with targets

The current British Government seems pretty good at setting targets. That is, it likes to specify, as clearly as possible, specific goals for public-sector institutions, such as schools, hospitals, and the police. Thus waiting lists, exam results, and crime statistics all have time-bound targets.

Various government ministers set targets for the number of people attending university, the percentage of those from working- and middle-class backgrounds or ethnic minorities, or females, or people with disabilities. Whatever.

And if you don't hit your targets, beware! It will be nicely reflected in your income. Miss your target and have your finances threatened. There may be carrots and/or sticks attached to target hitting or missing. Rewards for the successful, punishment for the failed. Just like the private sector. But the difference is that these targets are imposed by ideology, not by market forces. Indeed, political target setting is often an attempt to distort the market.

It's not difficult to set targets. It's harder to understand their consequences, both desirable and undesirable. Most work-related behaviors have multiple components. Emphasize one and the others become distorted.

Travel on a London bus and you'll be able to detect in seconds the major criteria by which drivers are rewarded. Watch people get on and flash their cards or tickets. Are they carefully inspected? Never. Do people get on without paying? Of course. Are there inspectors to check that people have paid? Possibly, but very few.

And people who run for the bus, or hobble along? They are ignored. And the safety and security of passengers with 'mobility needs'—the old, sick, buggy-steering? Forget it. No time for that. And jumping lights? Frequently. Almost as much as cyclists.

Why? Because the criterion is time. People complained that buses were late and infrequent. So the number of buses and bus lanes was increased, and drivers rewarded/ punished for keeping to time, or not. They have fewer excuses, so meeting the targets must be up to individual drivers.

Change the target to revenue received and you will have subway-like barriers, multiple inspectors, and more sensitive pricing. Make the success criterion safety and you get more cautious drivers, more inclined to obey traffic laws.

The issue is trade-off. And people will become immensely inventive to hit targets. Have hospital trolleys with easily removable wheels and instantly they become 'beds,' which fit criteria and fulfill targets.

Trains and airplanes have twigged the problem of on-time arrivals: simply change the time that the journey supposedly takes. Have you noticed that you can leave an hour late but still arrive on time. Tail winds? Extra weight on the accelerator? Of course not. A one-hour flight is now billed as a two-hour flight. It now takes twice as long by rail or car than it did 20 or even 40 years ago. But the airlines and trains are proud of their on-time performance.

And we all know, from bitter experience, the consequences of rewarding traffic wardens for each parking ticket issued. Their job is to promote traffic flow. To note and punish illegal parking, and possibly to check tax discs. Incentivize them exclusively for fining parking violations and they ticket ambulances, clamp fire engines, and issue penalty notices for utterly petty reasons. There are now websites dedicated to wrongfully issued tickets.

The moral of the story is simple. Set a clear target and, with enough incentive, people will certainly aim to hit it. But they will trade off, or sacrifice, other aspects of the job. Most jobs are multi-dimensional with multiple criteria. Choose one criterion or even two and you may well sacrifice others. Everything (well almost) can be done faster and made cheaper, but there is a cost. Setting targets can and does have unforeseen consequences.

This is not an argument against target setting, management by objectives—have your KRA, KPI, or whatever. But it is an argument against simply setting targets and neither giving help (rather than incentives) nor pondering their consequences. All good targets have multiple criteria relating to time, money, quantity, quality, and customer feedback. The trick is in specifying not just one or even two dimensions of the objective but understanding how the objective is met *and* how to help people achieve it better.

The unlearning organization

Do you recall the learning organization? It was the magic bullet of its time. Nearly 30 years ago a planning director of a large corporation argued in the *Harvard Business Review* that organizations, like people, had the capacity for learning and evolution.

Organizations could learn from their mistakes. But they had to capture their insights. They needed a memory and a way to get access to it. This might have inspired the concept of knowledge management.

Most people have had experience of the amnesic organization, where the same errors are made repeatedly. Or the ESN organization, which seems very slow to learn.

But is the problem learning or unlearning? Dennis Sherwood, an innovation guru, argues that certain organizational cultures seem powerfully against new ideas, practices, structures, and strategies. They have a problem letting go of the old and stopping doing what is familiar. If (and if only) the environment were stable; if things were like they have always been; if customers didn't change in their needs and expectations. If original processes and structures remained efficient … then no problem. But otherwise the unlearning, the anti-innovation, and the non-creative organizations become anachronistic, inefficient, and incompetent. In short, doomed.

What characterizes an unlearning organization? *First*, they see process, policies, and the like, as fixed not temporary. To be fit for purpose means being aware of sell-by dates. It means understanding that what works at one time (low inflation, minimal competition, key targets) does not necessarily work now. It means constant review to ascertain appropriateness, fitness, and efficiency. But unlearning organizations like rule-following not rule-breaking, continuity not change. And neither evolution nor revolution.

Second, the unlearning organization seems prepared to innovate only in the face of failure, even catastrophe. It stops gaps, makes and mends. It doesn't look to improve on processes, even when they work.

Third, it seems slow to praise but quick to chide. It seems not to realize that if things do not go according to plan this can be seen as a good learning opportunity, rather than a disappointing failure.

Fourth, the unlearning organization is driven by the tyranny of the urgent. It claims not to have time for imagining, for exploration, or for blue-sky thinking. If you don't put innovation, development, and progress in the diary, you won't get it.

Unlearning organizations are hard of hearing. Their customers and their staff give feedback, make suggestions, and point out problems. But no one is there to listen. The unlearning organization has no process to learn from its staff, by introducing tools such as climate surveys, and no forum to discuss and reward good ideas.

Unlearning organizations are often characterized by internal competition and secrecy rather than cooperation, openness, and sharing. Yes, you guessed it, they have silos not networks; staff don't see themselves as part of the organization as a whole; they don't like sharing information, resources, and especially risk.

Unlearning organizations default on no, nyet, it can't be done. They specialize in a range of expressions and phrases that are all pro status quo and anti-change. 'Let's try it,' 'Why not?' or 'Let's have a go' are not part of their vocabulary.

Unlearning organizations are super-good at evaluations and judgment. It may be one of the few things they really do quickly. But often too quickly. They know how to kill an idea before it has had time to develop. They know it is best to stop any innovation before it can become obviously appealing.

Unlearning organizations don't have innovation or creativity or imagination as competencies to be selected for, managed, or rewarded. Such attributes are not really seen as important. Indeed, they are often thought of as dangerous and undesirable.

Is the concept of innovation core to the organization? Does the board, the top team, or even senior management think it is central to their survival, competitive advantage, and future profitability? Is there a process to manage innovation? The answer in unlearning organizations is the ever familiar concept: NO!

Manager of special projects in an unlearning organization is a euphemism for the side-lined senior manager who won't go. The process of successful innovation requires the forming and managing of project teams tasked with driving the business. There is a skill to picking them and managing them that unlearning organizations never deliver.

But most of all the unlearning organization is characterized by pervasive risk aversion. The status quo is comfortable and apparently secure. The world is stable, predictable, and orderly. Alas, that is an illusion: the unlearning organization does risk badly. Its expectations of the success and failure of innovation are both wrong.

Three of the worst

There is now a growing literature on manager derailment, incompetence, and insanity. While magic-bullet, self-help books easily outsell books on failure, the latter do make fascinating reading.

One factor that differentiates the from sad/bad/mad managers is how they try to influence others. Persuading, motivating, and directing others (at all levels) is at the heart of the management enterprise. Good managers know this and they know how to do it. But bad managers rely too heavily on what are, in the long term, ineffective means.

The first inappropriate method is *intimidation*: the idea is to threaten or scare people into doing what one wants or, where appropriate, staying away. Excitable, unstable managers tend to be volatile, with sudden unpredictable outbursts of anger when things go wrong. Some go cold and uncommunicative once their orders have been barked out. Others are hypersensitive to questioning as if it is implied criticism. Still others are stubborn, procrastinating, and passive-aggressively resistant to reconsidering their position, their request, or their command.

Intimidators use rank or power to get their own way. They might do so, but with an excessive display of emotion or no emotion at all. They don't do rational argument, can be blinkered and selfish, and often make short-sighted, ill-considered decisions.

They can survive in hierarchical, risk-averse, slow-moving organizations like peace-time armies, process-oriented public-sector organizations, and the police. But they never really get on because they have few supporters or champions of their careers. Intimidation may work for short periods at odd times, but long term it's a real derailer.

The second ineffective method is *flattery, flirtation and seduction*. And this is certainly not the preserve only of women. The theatrical, attention-seeking drama queens of the business world try to persuade with their odd brand of 'charm.' Others do it with a sort of self-knowing charisma in the self-important belief that they are special and deserve others' total loyalty. A few like to play the 'wacky but brilliant' creative type, who has to be humored lest his/her juices dry up.

The flattering flirters are entertaining. If physically attractive and fairly senior they tend to get their way for a bit and with some people. But they are exploitative and frequently not close friends with the truth; hence their reputation for getting things done is not that great. The flirting method is just that. To flirt is to 'behave amorously but without serious intent.' Flirts flit from one person to another, trying but failing in their purpose.

The third method is to be *ingratiating*. This technique sometimes tries to reverse the leadership role. Some people try to gain favor with their staff by 'special treatment and favors.' Ingratiating managers very clearly 'put themselves out' for their staff, but then call in the favors … more and more often to atone for the initial gift.

Some ingratiators like to point out how weak they are, how difficult their job, how hard-working they have to be. Some even enjoy a sort of spurious victimhood in order to make their staff support them and work harder.

But these methods simply don't work. And they are often driven by personal pathology. The intimidating manager is often a selfish, conscienceless, disagreeable cynic. They just don't care about others. The flirtatious manager is often narcissistic with highly volatile mood swings. Fun at parties and presentations, but beware having one as your manager. And the ingratiating manager is often a coward.

Managers need to set expectations, clarify goals, and set targets. They need to help people achieve these targets with the right information, tools, and support. And staff need timely, accurate, and helpful information to assess how they are doing.

Trainer-mania

They are often an odd group of people, adult work-related trainers. They are not consultants, though many aspire to be because the daily rate is higher. They are not teachers, because that sounds patronizing to their clients. They are not lecturers, because that may either intimidate their clients or give the wrong impression of how they go about their business. And they are not coaches, though many are reinventing themselves as such.

Trainers are different. They tend to run short, skill-based courses. Training is meant to be practical, to yield results, to be relevant. It can be fun, but does not have to be. It can be both a reward and a punishment. It may be a requirement. It may be relatively easy or totally impossible to escape. It may be reserved for the young and naive employee, or a privilege of the senior, successful executive.

Trainers come in many guises, from the evangelical game show host to the belittling assassin. Some seem dependent on dreary manuals, while others think training is something between Disney and *American Idol*. People sort of 'drift into' training. Their backgrounds are often as varied as their styles, philosophy, and practice. Some seem like (failed but aspirant) actors; others disillusioned teachers. Many have a history of being made redundant.

Barriers to entry in the training business are low; qualifications seem to be optional. But training, like PR and advertising, is very sensitive to economic forces. While bull markets mean marvelous weekends at swish hotels playing foolish games, bear markets can involve mean pickings and empty diaries.

So there is much to worry and fret about. And there may

be, as a result, some very trainer-specific illnesses and problems. Consider the following semi-psychiatric conditions.

◆ *Chronic evaluation anxiety*: this occurs when the end-of-course 'happy sheets' really count. Good scores mean re-employment; bad scores mean 'thank you, but don't call us.' Trainers deal with this anxiety in many ways. Some try to fiddle the books by designing the feedback sheet themselves, delivering them at a particular high point in the proceedings, or quite simply pleading with the delegates. It's the only feedback that management receives, so it can count for a lot.

◆ *Intermittent entertainment confusion*: this is caused by not being sure to what extent one is trainer or entertainer. Happy sheet scores go up with funny anecdotes, amusing videos, and non-taxing games. They go down with tough assignments, the idea of end-of-course exams, and the trainer evaluating the delegates rather than the other way around. No-brainer, then. The pressure is to be funny, light, easy.

◆ *Periodic gadget fetish*: this is the false belief that delegates will be impressed by all sorts of odd gizmos that can be used in training. Quirky electronic goods are best. Playing whale music, or using subtly changing lights, or introducing aromatherapy-approved scents is the wacky, less electronic version of this fetish.

◆ *Naive luncheon compensation belief*: all trainers know the value of a good lunch. In fact the rank order of things that determine satisfaction with a one-day training course is probably: quality of lunch, party bag, networking card-exchange opportunity; famous people … then the content of the talks, and the nature of the training. Good lunches cost money. Uncontrollable elements come into play: hotels can be slow, vegetarians forgotten.

- *Adolescent manual disorder*: this is the paint-by-numbers, stick to the manual approach. It is the peculiar belief that manuals are like instruction kits that have to be followed logically and rigorously. It means the training is a dreary tramp through a tedious manual that pre- and proscribes everything.

- *Obsessive PowerPoint dependency*: this is akin to gadget fetish and is the belief that an arty-farty, eye-catching, cartoon-facilitated PowerPoint slide show is just the ticket. It is the peculiar belief that passive slide-watching has something to do with education.

- *Bipolar role-play exhibitionism*: a specialty of 'am dram' or television producer types, who encourage reluctant delegates to play outrageous parts while they are filmed using a cheap video camera. Sometimes trainers like to take part, doing the role play themselves.

- *Room layout fetish*: a faddish environmental-determinist notion that the way to place tables and chairs has an important effect on how the course goes. So there is 'cabaret,' with round tables to encourage interaction, and 'horseshoe' for trainer-led discussion.

- *Report-back poster dependency*: the idea that delegates can and should do all the work themselves by sitting around in breakout rooms filling flipcharts with inane drivel that they then feed back to the other groups. The idea is that a course is only really successful if every wall in the room is covered by these amateur posters.

- *Psychobabble test fixation*: this is a cheap time-filler that appeals to the self-absorbed narcissist. Make the dele-gates do some test, keep them in suspense, and feed back the results slowly, with great earnestness, and with a 'pseudo-concerned,' 'how fascinating' air. Lots of daft, time-absorbing exercises can easily be found to accom-pany the tests.

- *Habitual handout impulse*: this idea is to drip-feed material by a sort of session-at-a-time series of handouts. It creates a rhythm and delegates seem to value it more than getting the whole lot at once. Better still if handouts have to be processed before fitting into a folder.
- *Warm-up exercise mania*: this may be a protracted going-around-the-room either disclosing personal trivia or talking up one's job and company. On the other hand, it may involve high-school social games on the edge of litigation-worthiness.
- *Adolescent washup delirium*: this is the final session that may be a massive relief; a light-hearted affair dedicated mainly to trainers trying to increase their evaluation scores.

Typical and maximal performance

In the curious world of psychometrics, practitioners make a crucial distinction between tests of power and tests of preference.

Power tests are ability tests. They have different names—aptitude, cognitive ability, intelligence tests—but they tend to have three things in common. First, there are right/wrong, correct/incorrect answers. Second, most are timed. There is a time limit and many candidates do not finish in the time frame. Third, the questions become increasingly harder, starting off easy enough to encourage self-confidence, but soon becoming rather challenging.

Power tests have been around for over a century. They were devised to help those in education differentiate children according to the way in which they were best taught.

In business, more people use power tests for selection than any other type of test. Perhaps they know that intelligence is the single best individual difference predictor of success at work. And perhaps they also know that a half-hour of testing certainly goes a long way to improve the efficacy of the whole selection process.

The other kind of test—the preference test—comes in all shapes and sizes. Such tests purport to measure everything from personality to values, learning style to temperament. Preference tests tell you there are no right or wrong answers. Answer quickly and honestly. They are never timed. Indeed, it is fascinating to notice the differences in how people respond to these tests.

Preference tests are easy to construct but expensive to validate. They are everywhere: newspapers and magazines, the web and training courses. They range from the titillating 'Are you a demon or dodo under the duvet?' to the more tedious 'What is your supervisory style?'

The very large number of tests available makes consumers at once perplexed and wary. They know personality traits are important but they are quite rightly concerned by factors such as faking and circularity.

Another way of conceptualizing the preference/power distinction is the typical/maximal distinction. Preference tests are about how people typically behave. Indeed, questions are all about how one habitually or usually behaves in everyday social situations.

So the idea is that personality testing is about typical performance and intelligence testing about maximal performance. But is the job interview about typical or maximal performance? And what about the nature of work once one has got the job?

How typically do people behave in the job interview? Clearly both interviewer and interviewee are on their best behavior. Both do impression management. They strive to put their best foot forward, to show their best side, to shine. It is maximal, not typical.

In fact almost everything about behavior in the interview is exceptional. Dress, language, demeanor are special. That's why they can be exhausting. And that is why interviews have such poor predictive validity.

So the interview is about maximal performance: trying one's best to look good. In fact not being typical at all.

But what about working on the job? Another paradox. Do people work—in terms of their effort and ability—to the full, or just typically? Some always give their best.

Yet we know that many factors conspire to ensure that the quality and quantity of one's work is, well, pretty average. Very soon after getting a job one begins to work at the pace and style of the work group. When people are not aware they are being assessed, their productivity drops dramatically.

In one study people were tested on a supermarket checkout-type task. Their task was to process as many items as accurately and quickly as possible. It was a test of maximal performance and many did exceptionally well. Those that were hired to do the job were secretly recorded for a month or so and their typical rate measured. It tended to be around a third of that achieved on their testing day. So, paradoxically, tests of typical performance elicit maximal responses while tests of maximal performance can do a poor job at predicting typical performance.

That is precisely why people did and should use the concept of the *probationary period* to find out what a person is really like. People neither can, nor do, keep up appearances for six months. They act more naturally—typically. Their interpersonal interactions, rate of productivity, and self-confessed morale may still be subject to a little tweaking, but overall most can't keep up the pretence.

Furthermore, it may be of help to have those on probation rated by their peers and their customers. The whole 360-degree package. Why? Well, such people often get a better, more honest impression of how the employees really are. Warts and all, no make-up, little pretence.

Most people are worried about the validity of preference (personality) tests because of the possibility and probability of faking. Yet this occurs much more often in the interview than in the test.

To find out the abilities and preferences of people therefore is best done when they are acting typically—unmonitored for long periods of time. Slobs appear as slobs; the diligent as diligent. The problem, of course, is finding the best way to measure typical attitudes and performance.

SEX, VIOLENCE, AND CAR CHASES

Does sex sell? Ten years ago Calvin Klein launched a rather controversial and highly sexual advertising campaign that doubled sales of it's jeans. So is it a good idea to use sex (or violence) to help sales?

And we recently learnt that the 'Hello Boys' Wonderbra ads, that seem to be noticed more by guys who liked super-structure than the girls who have it, are to be changed. A more coy and functional approach seems to be in the offing.

There are various ways in which one can 'sex up' a product. Obviously one can use sexy ads. These may use highly attractive, scantily clad actors, or subtle innuendo, or not-so-subtle culturally understood images. Most of us remember speeding steam trains rushing into tunnels; the lady slipping a chocolate bar between her lips to the music of 'Je t'aime'; and suchlike.

Another way is to embed the advertisement in a sexy show. There are many post-9 PM watershed TV shows that deal with all aspects of sex … but not always sexily. And does one get more bang for one's buck if one places a sexy ad in a sexy show or an unsexy show?

The idea of commercial advertising is pretty simple: people see, listen to, or read an advertisement. They recall the brand, its strap-line, and the product. They later recognize the product in shops, on the web, or elsewhere, and buy it. They trust products more that have been advertised. Good ads lead to great sales.

But how does one get the ad noticed and remembered in the first place? Psychologists have known for half a century that memory for anything is dependent on how deeply the ad is 'processed.' People have to notice the ad, pay attention to it, understand the central message of it, and integrate it into their personal 'knowledge bank and system.' The more the advertisement catches their attention and interest the more they are likely to devote energy and capacity to processing it, and the stronger the memory trace will be.

If you like jargon you need to go through various stages: notice the ad; pay attention to the pictures, the words and the benefits; understand and comprehend that message, then integrate it into your knowledge bank, commercial schema, etc.

So ad agencies use drama, humor, sex, and violence to, they hope, make the ads more attention grabbing, interesting, and memorable. It is also hope that they will elicit emotions and mood states that enhance memory, though this may work only when that mood state occurs in the shopper.

People seem to like humor, some like sex, fewer like violence. But the job is selling products. Once the ad is made the question is where and when to show it. This depends mainly on costs, which depends on all sorts of thing—primarily (for TV) viewing figures.

But assume you have choice. You are marketing a food product. And you have made an outrageous, near-the-knuckle sexy ad. Do you slot it in a food show ad break, of which there are many, or in an auto show or a gardening show? Assume the same cost, the same viewers, the same readership. In other words, should one maximize program–advertisement congruity or incongruity?

A few American studies have looked at whether putting ads in a violent or sexual show improves or impairs memory for them. Three groups watched either a violent, sexually explicit, or neutral TV show that contained nine standard ads. Afterwards they were asked to recall the brands and identify them from pictures of similar brands on supermarket shelves. The next day they were each phoned and again asked to recall the brands. It was found that those watching the neutral show remembered most. Irrespective of their sex or age or how much they liked the show, the sexual and violent shows seemed to impair memory.

It may be that people attend more closely to sex and violence and then inevitably have less capacity to attend to other stimuli like ads. Also it is believed that sex and aggression in movies stimulate sexual and aggressive thoughts, which further limit interest in and attention paid to ads.

So the moral lobby of parents, priests, and pundits might not stem the flow of sex and violence on TV, but the advertising lobby that effectively subsidizes and therefore pays for the shows certainly will if it believes these results.

Uncertainty avoidance

After the Second World War, a group of American and German social scientists attempted to understand the 'mind of the Nazis.' They interviewed many of the major perpetrators, including Goering before he killed himself, to try to get an insight into 'what made them tick.'

The result of their efforts was a book called *The Authoritarian Personality*, which looked at the personality traits and processes associated with what might euphemistically be called 'interpersonal intolerance.' One trait that they identified was dubbed *intolerance of ambiguity*. It is now known as uncertainty avoidance or, more colloquially, 'managing the grey.' This has been identified as an important interpersonal, corporate, and cultural difference factor in business life.

All of us would like to be sure we live in a stable, predictable, just and certain world. Randomness, chaos, and capriciousness are truly terrifying, and we all invest a lot of energy trying to combat these forces of darkness. But our need for clarity, certainty, and decisiveness differs from individual to individual and country to country.

In Britain, there is no written constitution. In the law we muddle along on a case-by-case basis, eschewing any grand Code Napoleon. We positively revel in subtle meaningless differences like the 'Bishop of England' (York) versus the 'Bishop of All England' (Canterbury).

Uncertainty avoidance can be considered at the national, the organizational, and the individual differences level. The British can, it appears, cope with uncertainty. They are like the Indians and the Swedes and the Danes. But research indicates that other countries are rather different in this respect.

The Belgians and Japanese (no surprise there), the Greeks and the Portuguese have a stronger need to avoid uncertainty.

There are, it appears, all sorts of differences between low and high uncertainty avoidance cultures. Compared to those that score highly on uncertainty avoidance, cultures with lower scores are more accepting of dissent, more tolerant of deviance, more positive to the young, less risk averse, and less happy about showing emotion.

But organizations and industries can also be categorized on this dimension. Indeed, it is likely that the intolerant or uncertainty-avoiding seek out (and even seek to change) organizations that 'fit' with their own preferences. Again, researchers who have contrasted low and high uncertainty avoiding organizations see clear differences. The more tolerant tend to suffer less stress, live more in the present than the future, show less emotional resistance to change, and tend to have more highly achievement-motivated people. Tolerant companies tend to be smaller, with a smaller generation gap and a lower average age for higher-level jobs. The ethos is that managers should be selected on ability rather than seniority, that they need not be experts in the field they manage, and that generalists are preferable over specialists.

Organizations that do not have a problem with ambiguity and uncertainty seem to favor broad guidelines over clear requirements and instructions; they believe rules may be broken for pragmatic reasons and have no problem with conflict and competitiveness. More tolerant managers are more happy to delegate, compromise, and deal with 'foreigners' or people from other ethnic groups.

But it is not all good news for low uncertainty avoidance organizations. They tend to have higher labor turnover and the job satisfaction scores of people in them are lower. Managers report, and indeed have, less power. But they are much less bureaucratic.

Managers who have problems with uncertainty avoidance are afraid of, and made deeply uncomfortable by, uncertainty and ambiguity. People think of them as straightforward and predictable, though not creative. There are certainly areas of work where they will thrive—health and safety, production—but others where they would be deeply uncomfortable, like advertising or R&D.

Undercover marketing

This has been called guerrilla marketing, undercover marketing, and even viral marketing. It's an ideal essay topic for conspiracy theorists, the mildly paranoid, and the post-materialist post-capitalist.

The idea is this. We have learnt to retreat from, ignore, or 'turn off' the deluge of advertising we are faced with. We distrust and dislike media stars who peddle products at immense (and cynical) personal profit.

So marketers now employ a network of 'agents' to do their marketing. Who are they? Well, the usual suspects: hairdressers and bar staff, magazine journalists and DJs, waiters and webmasters, musicians and nightclub owners.

But they could be school prefects or popular kids. Or even teachers, nurses, or chemists. Anyone who dispenses information and advice. They don't have to be liked, well known, or important. They, it is argued, are the best word-of-mouth influences, the 'beamers of buzz.' It really is marketing at the grass roots. Marketing on the street.

How does it work? No real surprises. These 'ordinary' people with a useful consumer constituency are incentivized to push a brand or product. Nothing new there, then. But there are some innovative ideas. Attractive, undercover, but inevitably resting actors lean over bar counters and the like, calling loudly for certain brands. Actors are the fake tourists who get the real ones to take photos on their 'great new mobile phone.'

Of course, there have always been paid experts. But now there are crypto-focus groups. Participants are not there to provide information, but to be influenced by planted agents. There are also those 'sugging' (selling under the guise of) as opinion pollsters, whose aim is not so much to canvass as to change opinion.

Sometimes stunts are staged to get publicity and clever shots with logos. Young 'actors' pose on scooters outside places frequented by young people. Employees in CD and book stores pose as customers and strike up spontaneous conversations about particular 'must have' items.

Opinion leaders, local heroes, and community trendsetters are given products to 'test' (like cars) for a couple of months, and photographed regularly getting in and out of them. They provide the all-important 'social proof' of a product's worthiness.

Indeed, undercover marketers can conjure up 'flash mobs' to admire, praise, and purchase. Others turn into fake grassroots campaigners eager to picket and petition, boycott and boo. There are 'behalfers' who speak on behalf of the silent majority. They easily command airtime and column inches if they are articulate or curious. And that's seriously good publicity.

Undercover marketers are fascinated by contagion: the rapid, uncontrollable spread of habits, logos, and slogans. They want to infect others. They do so by targeting the 'coolest' and most influential industries. They hope to engineer word-of-mouth marketing and make it a science.

They have been known to study the tactics of cults, with their masterly control of their followers. *Behavioral* control of everything from food to finance, time-keeping to tooth brushing. *Information* control using clever but old-fashioned propagandist techniques. *Thought* control with thought-stopping chanting and meditation backed up by continual indoctrination. And *emotional* control, encouraging guilt, fear, phobias, and rollercoaster ups and downs.

And, if the conspiracy theorists are to be believed, the guerrilla marketers study the secrets of cults. Cults stress exclusivity (us who know the truth vs them), 'love-bombing' by instant friends and admirers, loaded language, relation-ship control, and good old-fashioned deception.

Some search the writings of the 'depth' psychologists for archetypes, images, and phrases that tap the great uncon-scious to find words to put into the mouths of our street actors.

Should you be paranoid? Is every mystery shopped a paid actor? Is your hairstylist, acupuncturist, or builder paid to recommend stores, products, and holiday resorts? Possibly not. But there is more undercover marketing about than ever.

Volunteering

One volunteer is worth ten conscripts. Some public-sector institutions rely very heavily on volunteers. Consider the local hospital and the range of people giving freely of their time and expertise. The visitors, the hospital radio, the charity store, and many others.

Why do they do it? How can they be encouraged and managed? Busybodies, do-gooders, and gong-chasers, or salt-of-the-earth, empathic, useful givers?

Where and when and how people volunteer may, in part, tell us why they volunteer. The school governor is different from the charity store attendant or the hospital radio announcer.

People volunteer to work in an organization because they have some allegiance to it. Kindness to a relative or oneself in hospital may provoke a sense of giving back in thanks. A person may volunteer to be a school governor, on the other hand, to attempt to improve the school's image, its facilities, or its standing for their own children.

Volunteers may treat their 'job' as a hobby, as a place to meet people, as an opportunity to keep one's hand in, or as a way of getting out more. They may be 'volunteered' by a spouse or encouraged by a friend—a rather oxymoronic form of volunteering.

But how does one manage voluntary workers or paid volunteers? What 'advertisements' do they respond to? And how can one manage them? Do you always have to ask volunteers if they will, want to, or feel like doing tasks?

Can one, or should one, try to manage, as opposed to organize, volunteers? Is life in the voluntary sector widely different from that in the public or private sector? The essence of the concept of voluntary is free will and free choice—acting without compulsion or payment. 'Of, subject to, and regulated by will,' as the dictionary puts it.

Volunteers can down tools, walk out, or throw their toys out of the crib quickly and with significant consequences. They may be no more temperamental than non-volunteers, but need careful management. So how to do it?

First, find their primary motive for volunteering. Is it social, ethical, even physical? Bear this in mind when allocating work. But it can be complicated: some don't want to be treated differently from non-volunteers, while others want a lot of acknowledgement for their 'selfless acts of giving.'

All work gives psychological benefits. It gives one a sense of purpose and an opportunity to exercise skills. It gives people a structure to their day, week, and year. It gives them an identity. And often, most of all, it gives them social contacts—with other workers, but also with customers and clients. Work, in short, is (often) good for you. But make sure you understand the benefits volunteers are deriving from it.

Second, have a more consultative and demographic style. Listen to volunteers' ideas: many have useful experience. Respect this, but always be clear what your primary task of being a manager is: setting clear goals, giving support to attain them, and consistent accurate feedback.

Third, remember that it is intrinsic, not extrinsic, rewards that are important. Volunteers may not be being paid but they are getting rewards. These rewards differ from individual to individual, and most may not always be entirely able to tell you.

Fourth, don't treat them differently—unless they very much want it. Integrate them into the workforce. Make sure they get a sense of community. Respect a sense of vocation— if they have one—but don't highlight it in front of others.

Fifth—and this may sound contradictory—just practice

good management. Set people clear tasks. Let them know what they should be doing (how, when, and why) and give praise when it is done.

Could or should one have one of those government-ordained tsars: a voluntary-sector tsar? Perhaps, but this could easily lead to revolution. The voluntary sector is highly heterogeneous. People are inspired by *ideology* (both religious and political), by *personal experience* and by *need to volunteer*. There are also considerable differences within voluntary organizations as to why people are there.

They need, like everyone else, good management. But most of all they need perceptive managers—managers with that conceptually elusive quality called emotional intelligence as well as good business savvy.

Work and longevity

What makes for a happy, healthy, independent old age? Why do some people look finished at 50 while others remain snappy at 70 or energetic at 80? Is it all in your genes or your lifestyle? More likely it is a combination of both.

Yes, longevity runs in families. You certainly inherit dispositions and traits, but lifestyle does make a difference. And what determines lifestyle? A mixture of work and leisure pursuits.

Some years ago David Kaun, an epidemiologist from the University of California, did a fascinating study on the longevity of artists—from architects to writers, composers to conductors, painters to photographers. He followed a tradition of life insurance studies that examined the longevity of professional groups from scientists to journalists.

The results of the study gave rise to the title of the piece: 'Writers Die Young' (*Journal of Economic Psychology*, Vol. 12). In fact writers, whose mean age of death was only 61.7 years, lived ten years less than most of the other groups.

But why? Stress? Unlikely. In books that rank-order occupational stress, writers appear much lower down the scale than architects, conductors, actors, and dancers. The most stressed jobs were fire-fighter, racing car driver, astronaut, surgeon, and professional footballer.

So what's the answer? One approach is to look at *hedonic calculus*. This is working out the pleasure received, on a day-to-day basis, from a person's work and non-work (leisure) activities. People at work can derive pleasure (and pain) from both the product and the process. That is, at least for arty-farty types, what they are trying to achieve (the painting, the opera, the score, the book, the performance) and how they go about achieving it.

So what is it about writing that seems to reduce life expectancy? *First*, for novelists (as opposed to journalists, and even poets) the product is often a (very) long time in completion. Yes, there are exceptions—Anthony Burgess, Barbara Cartland—but most writers seem happy with 500–800 words per day. Hemingway set a target of 500, Graham Greene 800. At that rate it may take one to two years to produce a 50,000–60,000-word novel. Artists, composers, and sculptors all have a much greater output.

Second, writing is a painful, lonely process. It is difficult, demanding, and unsatisfying. The writer needs imaginary inspiration, excitement, but is all too often confronted by the tyranny of the blank page or screen. The writer needs self-confidence, energy, and a curiosity about people. Musicians practice with others. Dancers, singers, and photographers shoot the breeze, practice and interact with each other daily—sometimes out of necessity, sometimes choice.

Many writers take to drink to sharpen the 'dull flatness' of the typical day, as Faulkner puts it. Alcohol can fuel the imagination, and increase self-confidence. It certainly does not help architects, dancers, or conductors. One might 'come down' with drink in the performing arts, but never use it to get the juices going. And as we know, drink is addictive.

Artistic people have a preference for impromptu, free, unstructured activities. They like disorderly non-conformity. They like the quirky, the impulsive, and the emotional. But great art requires discipline. A lifestyle (leisure activities) that is not compatible with your chosen career of necessity requires a change in one or the other. Dancers and singers have to stay fit. But perhaps writers' legendary consumption of drink and drugs can, for a time, be compatible with their trade. Their risk-taking, high-excitement leisure activities—like hunting, fast cars, and faster women—may help the boredom and pain, but lead to a shortened life.

What are the implications for the rest of us? First, your

work and leisure activities affect your mental and physical welfare, and hence longevity. Some leisure choices that seem to complement work are not conducive to a happy life. Make sure you find a source of regular immediate pleasure at work, such as employing the company of others. Set goals to give a sense of achievement. Make your leisure support, not sink, your career.

Work bribes and incentives

Money motivates, right? Parents bribe their children with pocket money, candy, clothes, and the latest electronic gadgets to try to get them to work harder at school. Nothing new in that. Nothing wrong in that?

Now businesses, schools, and governments have got in on the act. Good behavior is monetarily rewarded; bad behavior punished by lack of reward.

In the UK, schools have promised exotic vacations or four-figure sums to pupils who do well in exams. It seems to make good economic sense. Good grades improve school ratings, which attract more money, which can be spent on getting better grades. Virtuous cycles. Driven by money.

And organizations have taken to the 'no claims bonus' concept, so beloved by the insurance industry. This is clearly manifest in the attendance arena. The problem of absenteeism is being dealt with by incentives. Take no or few days off and you get some incentive, possibly cash.

A sensible punishment to the work-shy and a just reward to the conscientious, or an inequitable, unjust, and immoral punishment of the sick? Certainly the causes, consequences, and cures of absenteeism are a hot topic. It has deep ideological correlates. For those who believe we are now willing slaves of tyrannical task masters, the idea of rewarding people for attendance says that is all they are about. Overwork makes one sick, sickness leads to absence, and now additionally to poverty.

But the incentive strategy has other problems. It is all about the messages it sends. Psychologists have distinguished between intrinsic and extrinsic motivation and satisfaction.

Intrinsic motivation refers to the pleasure one gets from the activity itself. Most of us can name activities that give joy, that give one the experience of 'flow', that are so captivating time passes unnoticed. Work becomes play if one is intrinsically motivated. Artisan creators like potters and painters know this.

Extrinsic motivation has little or nothing to do with the activity itself. Indeed, we have the concepts of compensation (and benefits). That is, the activity may be dull, dangerous, and total drudgery, but the money makes up for it. Everyone has their price, and the job market has prices for every job. Of course, many factors—like skill, knowledge, responsibility, and scarcity—determine pay.

But we do know that paying people for an activity actually changes their attitude to that activity. There are two schools of thought on this issue. The first says that money is just one of a number of fairly equivalent types of incentive. You can change behavior by judicious application of reward and punishment like giving, withholding, or indeed taking money. Money can be a carrot or a stick. It works well to shape behavior.

The other school puts forward a more complex and counterintuitive argument. It argues that, if you pay people to be creative, they become less so because they then work according to different criteria. They believe they are working at creative tasks and being paid accordingly, as opposed to exploring radical ideas and processes.

They would argue that if you pay people to get good exam results you reduce the pleasure in learning, understanding, and thinking. Worse, you set up a sort of economic dependency model where nothing is done except for money. Hence the idea of knowing the price of everything and the value of nothing.

There is all the difference in the world between a prize and an incentive. Prizes are public testaments of worth. They can have little monetary value. Scientists work for the Nobel Prize, not the dosh that goes with it. If they wanted the money they would probably have become business men and women.

If you pay people not to be absent, they adopt the philosophy of presenteeism. You want people to want to go to work, to enjoy the activity, to rejoice in exploring and exploiting their particular talents.

So beware the *homo economicus* fallacy. Rewarding people monetarily for how you want them to behave could have serious deleterious long-term effects on how they approach their work.

Work is good for you

In the UK, the government's Work and Pensions Secretary wants many of the 2.8 million claimants of incapacity benefit to go back to work. His claim is that work is better for people than daytime television. Rather than cause stress and depression, work has the opposite effect. Cynical political posturing aimed at reducing the £12.5 billion bill, or evidence-based science?

Studies of the psychological benefits of work date back to at least the 1930s. By studying those who are out of work, by accident or design, social scientists have understood why, when, and how work can be good for you. By looking at the lives of those in times of high unemployment, at accident victims, and those who have retired, it is possible to see the psychological effects of worklessness.

There are at least five documented benefits of work, other than the money it brings in. First, work gives a sense of structure and purpose. People like routine as long as it is not too rigid. They like patterns and rhythm and predictability. Work gives a shape to the day, the week, the month. Periods of prolonged worklessness lead to a loss of the sense of time, of extended and restless sleep.

We are complex social animals. A major benefit of work is our friendship network in the workplace. Work colleagues are often a source of social support and great interest. People like to shoot the breeze at the start of the day: talk about last night's TV or dinner conversations. They like to compare notes on how they see the world, on what they feel in the face of events both in and out of the workplace. Worklessness leaves people feeling isolated, forgotten, and friendless.

Third, work gives a sense of social identity. For men especially, who you are is what you do. Hence all the fuss when job titles are changed. Many of us define ourselves in terms of the exact job we do and the organization we work for. Despite the fact that, for many, being on benefit has lost its stigma it still implies another loss.

Next, work can provide a real sense of achievement and of mastery. We all have talents and skills, and it is often work that channels these most efficiently. We know it is artisans— such as artists, potters, and gardeners—who have the highest job satisfaction because so much of themselves is in their work. People out of work tend not to exploit their talents.

And work keeps you physically and mentally active. Physiotherapists and osteopaths used to recommend bed rest for many skeletal problems. They now do the precise opposite. The accumulating evidence is that back and other problems are improved by exercise and movement, not the other way around.

So there are latent benefits of work that would no doubt improve both the physical and mental health of many inca-pacity claimants. But there are good jobs and bad jobs in terms of the number and type of the benefits they provide. Badly paid, anti-social, low-status, menial jobs are unlikely to provide many benefits. And it may be that a dispropor-tionate number of claimants indeed held this type of job.

Occupational therapy used to be seen as applying to those with severe disabilities though accident, trauma, or birth. People were taught new skills in line with their disabilities. This was known to have major psychological benefits for the individual, and to be a wise investment for institutions like hospitals and jails. Perhaps what claimants need is an occu-pational therapy assessment and then some help to get jobs that will indeed reduce the ennui that goes with long-term worklessness.

About the author

Adrian Furnham is Professor of Psychology at University College, London, UK. He is on the editorial board of a number of journals, has received many awards and was recognized as the most productive psychologist in the world from 1985 to 2000. He is the author of over 700 journal articles and more than 55 books, including several, successful, popular management books. He acts as a consultant to a number of bodies including HM Government, British Airways, HBOS and SAP, and also a number of multinational corporations. He writes regular columns in the *Daily Telegraph* and *The Sunday Times* and is a frequent contributor to BBC radio and television.

ALSO BY ADRIAN FURNHAM

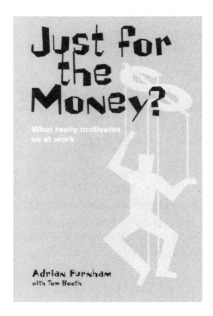

How many people work just for the money? What is your time actually worth? How does your organization handle the trade-off between the good, the cheap and the fast? These are some of the questions asked by Adrian Furnham and Tom Booth, the authors of this thought-provoking book. *Just for the Money?* challenges our assumptions about money in the workplace, at home and in our daily lives.

ISBN 9781904879503 / £9.99 Paperback

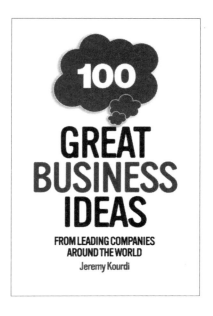

In the world of business, new ideas and energy are needed constantly – in many ways and at varying times – to ensure success. This book contains 100 insightful and useful business ideas that will help you succeed.

Written in a stimulating and flexible way, *100 Great Business Ideas* contains ideas with proven power and potency that actually work. The ideas are varied, interesting, and thought-provoking, and some of the best ideas used in business. Some are simple – sometimes almost embarrassingly so – while others are based on detailed research and brilliant intellect.

ISBN 9781905736072 / £8.99 Paperback

The Six Fundamentals of Success Stuart R. Levine

The rules for getting it right for yourself and your organization

We all have our own ways of working. But if you look at people who excel, you'll spot certain similarities. They know how to set priorities, and make a point of tackling the most important tasks first. They always work with a sense of urgency. They can sum up in a sentence or two how their business stands out from the pack. Qualities like these never go out of style; on the contrary, they are central to any successful career. Adopt them, and you and your company have a better chance of getting ahead.

Aimed at managers and entrepreneurs at every level in companies large and small, *The Six Fundamentals of Success* provides a clear-headed, readable guide to help people and businesses thrive in today's challenging climate.

ISBN 9781904879176 / £8.99 Paperback

OTHER ADVICE AND IDEAS FOR THE HUNGRY MIND

In this unique and bestselling book, Harro von Senger shows today's managers:

- How to successfully resist crafty manoeuvres and tricky attacks.
- How to avoid being outsmarted during negotiations.
- How to use the 36 Stratagems to one's own advantage without conflicting with the legal and moral order.

The 36 Stratagems can become an everyday work tool for managers, a permanent source of inspiration, and a globally useful approach to solving and avoiding problems. Moreover, this is an indispensable book for all those trying to understand China and the Chinese people, especially in business matters.

ISBN 9781904879503 / £14.99 Hardback

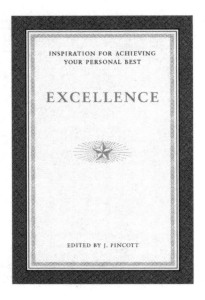

In every profession are people whose lives are distinguished by true excellence. Think of the Dalai Lama, Toni Morrison, Steven Spielberg, Susan Sarandon, Warren Buffett, Sergey Brin and Larry Page. How did they get to greatness?

This book is a collection of more than 300 quotes and passages on excellence from some of the world's most fascinating thinkers and leaders. Thematically organized as a handbook of little lessons, *Excellence* touches upon passion, creativity, discipline, ethics, flexibility, intuition, and incisiveness. Here is a guide for all who strive to achieve their personal best.

ISBN 9781904879893 / £9.99 Hardback